Trade Liberalisation, Economic Growth and Environmental Externalities

Hansa Jain

Trade Liberalisation, Economic Growth and Environmental Externalities

An Analysis of Indian Manufacturing Industries

palgrave
macmillan

Hansa Jain
Sardar Patel Institute of Economic
and Social Research
Ahmedabad, Gujarat, India

ISBN 978-981-10-2886-1 ISBN 978-981-10-2887-8 (eBook)
DOI 10.1007/978-981-10-2887-8

Library of Congress Control Number: 2016956867

Printed on acid-free paper

This Palgrave Macmillan imprint is published by Springer Nature
The registered company is Springer Nature Singapore Pte Ltd.
The registered company address is: 152 Beach Road, #22-06/08 Gateway East, Singapore 189721, Singapore

Preface

Trade liberalization measures initiated in India during 1991 were focused on manufacturing industries. It was considered that the manufacturing industries, due to its strong inter-sectoral linkages, have the capacity to stimulate the growth of other sectors. As a result, the liberal trade policies that involved reduction in trade barriers, inflows of FDI, capital and technologies were adopted to increase the manufacturing output; however, these measures were more inclined towards those industries whose products have greater demand in developed countries. The improved access to capital and technology from abroad has restructured the Indian manufacturing industries. As a result, India's revealed comparative advantage was altered. India, which was earlier the exporter of primary goods, has now become the exporter of finished goods. This indicates that India has now become the production base for the developed countries, which implies that it has to bear all the positive and negative effects of production activities. Positive effect arises when the imported technologies, exposure to knowledge and ideas have spillover effect. Negative effect arises, when the industrial pollution adversely affects the social well-being. Since the market fails to capture these effects, they are referred to as externalities. Under the ambit of liberal trade measures, the probability of environmental externalities increases when there is a difference in the environmental standards between the developed and developing countries.

This study is undertaken in two parts. The first part examines the trade-induced structural changes in the Indian manufacturing industries since 1991. The second part determines the environmental externalities (in terms of pollution loads) of each manufacturing industry and its relation with the manufacturing output, changing composition and technology. In a way, the study tries to capture the impact of trade-induced manufacturing growth on environmental externality by decomposing the total effect into scale, composition and technique effects. Apart from the manufacturing activity, the study incorporates the effect of other factors that improves with the process of economic growth. Further, the impact of these environmental externalities is estimated on the well-being of local population. Local population here means the population in the surrounding of industrial set-up in a radius of 10 km.

In the race of achieving a higher economic gain and competing with the world producers, the quality of environment is always neglected. Rather the environmental quality is treated as luxurious as it involves cost of abatement measures. The study considers that the inefficiencies in production processes generate negative environmental externality. The study comes out with some alternative measures that would increase the production efficiency on the one hand and increase the social well-being on the other.

This study is an outcome of the research project funded by Indian Council of Social Science Research (ICSSR). I gratefully acknowledge the ICSSR for endorsing me such an important study.

I am indebted to Sardar Patel Institute of Economic and Social Research for providing me an apt atmosphere and support to carry this research. I am equally thankful to Prof. Niti Mehta, Director of the Institute, for smoothening the process for this study. I also acknowledge the timely support provided by the Institute's staff. My special thanks are to Dr. R.R. Bhatnagar and Dileep Singh for managing the task.

My sincere thanks are to the officials at the district headquarters, panchayat offices, village sarpanch, doctors at primary health centres, school teachers of the selected villages and stakeholders for providing me the valuable inputs.

The results of this study were presented in seminars and conferences. I sincerely acknowledge the comments and suggestions given by Professors G.K. Chaddha, Ghanshyam Singh and A.K. Singh. I am equally grateful to Prof. Anju Kohli for discussion and providing useful comments during the progress of this work.

Lastly, I wish to thank my family for providing me the moral support.

Contents

List of Abbreviations

ASI	Annual Survey of Industries
ATC	Agreement on Textiles and Clothing
BOD	biological oxygen demand
CDF	cumulative distribution function
CFC	chlorofluorocarbon
CO	carbon monoxide
CO_2	carbon dioxide
CPCB	Central Pollution Control Board
CUTS	Consumer Unity and Trust Society
DGCIS	Directorate General of Commercial Intelligence and Statistics
DIPP	Department of Industrial Policy and Promotion
DTAA	Double Taxation Avoidance Agreement
EDGAR	Electronic Data Gathering, Analysis and Retrieval System
EKC	Environment Kuznet Curve
EME	emerging market economies
ERP	Effective Rate of Protection
ESG	environmentally sensitive goods
FDI	foreign direct investment
FEH	factor endowment hypothesis
FEMA	Foreign Exchange Management Act
FERA	Foreign Exchange Regulation Act
FICCI	Federation of Indian Chambers of Commerce and Industry
FP	fine particulates
GDP	gross domestic product
GPN	global production network
GVA	gross value added
HOS	Heckscher–Ohlin–Samuelson

HT	high technology
IEM	Industrial Entrepreneurs Memorandum
IMF	International Monetary Fund
IPPS	Industrial Pollution Projection System
ISIC	International Standard Industrial Classification
JV	joint venture
LDC	less developed countries
LT	low technology
MHT	medium high technology
MLT	medium low technology
MNC	multinational corporation
NAFTA	North American Free Trade Agreement
NCAER	National Council of Applied Economic Research
NIC	National Industrial Classification
NO_2	nitrogen dioxide
NO_x	nitrogen oxide
NRI	non-resident Indian
OECD	Organisation for Economic Co-operation and Development
OGL	Open General License
OLM	ordinal logit model
OPEC	Organization for Petroleum Exporting Countries
PHH	pollution haven hypothesis
PLUM	polytomous universal model
POL	petroleum, oil and lubricants
QR	quantitative restriction
R&D	research and development
RBI	Reserve Bank of India
RCA	revealed comparative advantage
REP	replenishment
SEBI	Securities and Exchange Board of India
SIA	Secretariat for Industrial Assistance
SO_2	sulphur dioxide
SPM	suspended particulate matter
SPSS	Statistical Package for the Social Sciences
TPRI	Trade Policy Review India
TSP	total suspended particulates
TSS	total suspended solids
UAE	United Arab Emirates
UK	United Kingdom
US	United States
VOC	volatile organic compound
WTO	World Trade Organization

List of Figures

List of Tables

CHAPTER 1

Introduction

Abstract The liberal trade policies that involved reduction in trade barriers and facilitated inflows of foreign direct investment, capital and technologies restructured the Indian manufacturing industries. Apart from the difference in factor endowments, the comparative advantage nowadays is seen in terms of environmental regulatory gaps between the trading partners. This raises the concern whether trade-induced production structure of Indian manufacturing industries is generating environmental externality. This study is endeavoured to explore the relationship between trade liberalization, economic growth and environmental externalities by taking the case of Indian manufacturing industries. This chapter gives an overview of the subject, statement of the problem, objectives and scope of the study.

Keywords Introduction · Objectives · Hypothesis · Scope of the study

Trade liberalization in India was intended to free the manufacturing sector from the barriers to entry as well as from other restrictions related to expansion, diversification and modification with the aim to improve its efficiency, productivity and competitiveness.[1] It was believed that the growth of manufacturing sector would correct the balance of payment deficit by promoting exports on the one hand and develop other sectors through its inter-sectoral linkages on the other. A liberal trade policy by facilitating

H. Jain, *Trade Liberalisation, Economic Growth and Environmental Externalities*, DOI 10.1007/978-981-10-2887-8_1

inflows of capital, investment and technologies alters the production structure in manufacturing industries in a manner that depends on the nation's comparative advantage. Apart from the differences in factor endowments, the comparative advantage, nowadays is seen in terms of environmental regulatory gaps between the trading partners.[2] If the stricter environmental regulation increases the relative cost of production for polluting industries, one would expect them to relocate to countries that have laxer regulation.[3]

India's major trading partners are the developed countries of the world. These developed countries generally keep their environmental standards high while India has weak compliance with environmental regulations. This raises the concern that whether the trade-induced production structure of Indian manufacturing industries is generating environmental externality. If it is so, how far these externalities are influencing the human well-being?

1.1 Trade Liberalization and Economic Growth

Trade liberalization, nowadays, is considered to be the engine of economic growth. The advocates of free trade suggests that it maximizes the world output, enlarges the consumption capacities, provides access to scarce resources and worldwide markets for products, enhances skill and technical know-how, develops managerial talents, entrepreneurial capacity, fosters healthy competition, increases real income and capital accumulation and checks inefficient monopolies. Globalization combined with trade liberalization encourages exports and imports and also increases incentives for investment and innovation. It also encourages foreign direct investment (FDI) which supplements domestic investment and leads to higher growth of the economy (Bhalla 2008). Globalization, with domestic liberalization, reduces the power of trade unions and unnecessary lock-outs. As a result, the manufacturing sector grows without hindrances. Thus all the participating countries are benefitted from free trade provided their resource allocation follows revealed comparative advantage, to choose industries in accordance with relative international prices, so that industrialization everywhere is part of an optimal division of labour between countries in the world economy (Nayyar 2011).

Dating back to the writings of classical economists (1730–90), Adam Smith (1776) stressed the importance of trade as a vent for surplus production and as a means of widening the market, thereby improving the division of labour and also the level of productivity. David Ricardo, 'on the assumptions of perfect competition and full employment of resources, showed that the countries can realize welfare gains by specializing in the production of those goods that have the lowest opportunity cost[4] and trading the surplus of production over domestic demand, provided that the international rate of exchange between commodities lies between the domestic opportunity cost ratios' (Thirlwall 2000). Malthus perceived the contribution of trade in the growth process to be one of offsetting diminishing returns in agriculture and increasing the labour supply by affecting the work-leisure choice. International trade expands the consumption set by making available foreign goods and, therefore encourages people to increase their work effort at any given wage rate (Acharyya 2013). As per the neo-classical economists, as international trade raises the real income of trading nations, it allows for higher rate of savings, capital formation and therefore output growth. On the other hand, the redistribution effect of trade alters the rate of output growth if people have different marginal propensities to save.

'Generalized trade liberalization in the form of unilateral tariff reductions (or the reduction of non-tariff barriers to trade) improves growth performance (Thirlwall 2000). Export growth relaxes the balance of payments constraint on demand by providing foreign exchange to pay for import content of higher level of consumption, investment and government expenditure. Most developing countries are constrained in their growth performance by a shortage of foreign exchange and could therefore grow faster with more exports' (Thirlwall 2000). Experiences show that after adapting trade liberalization and opening the economy for the world, there has been manifold increase in world trade relative to world output. While world output (or gross domestic product) has expanded fivefold, the volume of world trade has grown 16 times at an average compound rate of just 7 per cent per annum (Ogunrinola 2013). In some individual countries, notably in Southeast Asia, the growth of export has exceeded 10 per cent per annum. Exports have tended to grow faster in countries having more liberal trade regimes, and these countries have evidenced the fastest growth of GDP. In this sense, Marshall advocated that it is difficult, if not impossible, to understand the growth and development process of countries without reference to their trade performance (Thirlwall 2000).

Empirically, there are static gains[5] from trade that arise from reallocation of resources from one sector to another as increase in specialization based on comparative advantage takes place. These are the trade creation gains that arise within customs unions or free trade areas as the trade barriers are removed between members, but the gains are once-for-all. There are also dynamic gains from trade as the export market widens the total market for a country's producers. Moreover, the liberal trade is associated with stimulus to competition, more investment and faster productivity growth based on scale economies, capital flows, learning by doing, the acquisition of new knowledge, ideas and dissemination of technical knowledge through FDIs and changes in attitudes and institutions. The essence of dynamic gain is that they shift outwards the production possibility frontier by augmenting the availability of resources for production through increasing the productivity of resources and increasing the quantity. In the context of 'new' growth theory,[6] these are all forms of externalities which keep the marginal product of physical capital from falling, so that trade improves the long-run growth performance of countries. The exposure to foreign competition confers externalities on the non-export sector also.[7] This accelerates the overall economic growth. Concern with economic growth, meanwhile, is resurgent, as is evidenced by Romer (1986), Lucas (1988), Stokey (1988) and many others. Much of this work emphasizes on the role of external increasing returns. This implies that investment in capital by one agent improves the productive efficiency of all. This 'new growth theory' relies on positive externalities to generate growth, but does not consider that the negative externalities to growth may also affect the growth process. The increase in competition (as reflected in the reductions in price-marginal cost mark-ups), via trade liberalization, brings additional gains by reducing the deadweight losses created by domestic monopolies and oligopolies (Krishna and Mitra 1998).

1.2 Trade-Induced Growth and Environmental Externalities: Emerging Issues in Developing Economies

Liberalized trade policy has transformed the production pattern as well as the composition of trade of countries all over the world. Previously, the developing countries that were recognized in terms of the exporter of primary goods to developed countries have now become the importer of primary and intermediary goods, capital and technology from developed countries. On the other hand, the developed countries that were exporting manufactured goods to developing countries are now importing manufactured goods from developing countries. This implies that developing countries have now become production base for many of the manufactured goods of the world.

Trade liberalization changes key supply cost of the producers in developing countries relative to those in developed countries, leading to possible changes in composition in industrial production and exports at domestic front in developing countries.

In order to have higher economic growth, developing countries are engaged in more trade-related activities, particularly in production of export goods. More trade probably means more production, and more production historically meant more pollution. The comparative advantage of freer trade can be seen in terms of differences in factor endowment and environmental standards between the developed and developing countries. Taking the case of India, based on 'traditional' factor endowments such as capital and labour, India's comparative advantage is in labour-intensive production. Therefore, based on the factor endowment hypothesis (FEH), it could be expected that with a move towards freer trade, India should increase its specialization in labour-intensive production. However, the evidence that India has a story of poor enforcement of and weak compliance with environmental regulation counters the prediction of the factor endowment effect. If less strict environmental policies do influence production decisions, 'environment' can be considered as non-traditional factor of production, and India may have an advantage in pollution-intensive production (Jha and Rabindran 2004). This generates a negative externality – costs that are inflicted upon the society but are not internalized by the private agent. Consequently, the private cost of production remains far below the social cost of production. This results into overestimation of the economic growth.

On the contrary, advocates of freer trade argue that increase in trade-driven economic growth has positive environmental externalities in the long run. Income growth results in a higher demand for better environmental quality (such as cleaner air and drinking water) which, in turn, induces the local government to set higher environmental standards for domestic producers and implement pollution abatement rules more strictly. With increase in income, more resources can be spared for environmental protection. Countries that are more open to trade can adopt cleaner technology more quickly (WTO 2004).

The studies have related the economic growth and environmental externalities[8] in three ways: (a) Greater economic activities raises the demand for all inputs including environment as free input and, hence, increases emissions. This is the *scale effect.* (b) If people increase their demand for clean environment as their income rise, they will then tolerate higher levels of pollution only if effluent charge is higher. Since higher effluent charges encourage firms to shift towards cleaner production process, this *technique effect* tend to reduce emission. (c) If income growth shift preferences towards cleaner goods, i.e., if clean goods are relatively income elastic, then the share of pollution-intensive goods in output will decrease. This *composition effect*, therefore, tend to decrease emissions. It is to be noted here that this composition effect of growth is demand-driven rather than production-driven as in the case of the short-run effect of trade liberalization (Acharyya 2013).

At low levels of development, both quantity and the intensity of environmental degradation are limited to the impacts of subsistence economic activity on the resource base and to limited quantities of bio-degradable wastes. As agriculture and resource extraction intensity and industrialization takes off, both resource depletion and waste generation accelerate. At higher levels of development, structural change towards information-based industries and services, more efficient technologies and increased demand for environmental quality result in levelling-off and a steady decline of environmental degradation (Panayotou 1993).

1.3 Conceptual Framework

Trade liberalization consists of policies aimed at opening up the economy to foreign investment and lowering trade barriers by way of tariff reduction (Chakraborty 2012). Post-liberalization phase was marked with dismantling of controls (i.e. privatization) and import liberalization. The licensing system was done away with to a large extent (Bhat 2013).

Globalization means gradual integration of economies through free movement of goods, services and capital. Globalization has progressed with greater speed since the beginning of the 1980s and most of the countries of the world have been more closely integrated with one another since then. The process of integration has been greatly facilitated because of declining transport costs and the introduction of information and communication technologies (ICTs). Simultaneously, gross trade, FDI, capital flows and technology transfers have risen significantly (Bhalla 2008)

Trade-related industrial pollution: The relationship between trade expansion and environmental protection has been characterized by two extreme viewpoints – promoting trade worsens environmental conditions and higher environmental standards impose an economic cost (Jaffe et al. 1995). On this basis, Jaffe et al. (1995) proposed two competing hypothesis.

Pollution haven hypothesis (PHH) is derived from changes in environmental legislation that in turn can distort existing patterns of comparative advantage. Stringency of environmental regulations increases with income. This implies that in the developed world, the cost of complying with the environmental regulations should be greater in comparison to the developing countries. In other words, one can assume that developing countries possess a comparative advantage in pollution-intensive production. Thus, there is a high probability for arising of 'pollution havens' in developing countries. This itself shows that on behalf of liberalized trade policies, the pollution-intensive industries might relocate in developing countries. *Factor endowment hypothesis* (FEH), predicts that trade liberalization will result in trade patterns consistent with the Heckscher–Ohlin–Vanek (HOV) theory of comparative advantage based on factor endowment differentials. Rich countries are typically well endowed with physical capital. Since capital-intensive goods are often also pollution-intensive, factor endowment theories of international trade predict that rich countries specialize in polluting goods. Rich countries have higher willingness to pay for environmental quality (Mukhopadhyay and Chakraborty 2005)

An **externality** is said to exist if an economic agent (like an individual or a firm) is affected by the economic activity of others without the benefit of a market to mediate between them (Neher 1990). Externalities play a crucial role in environmental economics. When firms in a market economy make decisions regarding what to produce and how much to produce, they normally take into consideration the price of what they will produce and the cost of items for which they will have to pay: labour, raw materials, machinery, energy and so on. These are private costs of a firm. A profit maximizing firm will try to keep its private costs as low as possible. Sometimes, there are costs associated with an economic activity that are borne by the population at large but do not appear in the calculations of the producer. Similarly, there might be benefits accruing to the society that the producer fails to capture. In the presence of externality, there is a divergence between private and social costs and benefits. Private costs underestimate (overestimate) social costs if the externality is negative (positive). The presence of adverse (negative) externality, in many production operations imposes the external costs – external because although they impose real costs on the society, firms do not normally take them into account when they decide about output rates. These are costs that are external to the firms but internal to the society as a whole. One of the major types of external cost is the cost inflicted on people through environmental degradation. When private costs diverge from social costs, price determined in a competitive market fails to reflect the social cost and, therefore, cannot act as the right signal for producers and consumers.

1.4 Statement of the Problem

The economic reforms initiated by the Indian government since 1991 have had a strong industry focus, with the manufacturing sector being viewed as a vehicle of growth in the changed milieu (Rajakumar 2011). The policy changes included the dismantling of industrial licensing, de-reservation of industries for public sector, relaxing of restrictions on industrial investment and expansion, disinvestment of government equity in public sector enterprises and opening up of industries for FDI. It was held that the lesser control associated with substantial degree of openness of the economy through trade flows, investment flows, technology flows and capital flows would increase productivity of the Indian manufacturing industries by improving efficiency and increasing competitiveness. This compelled the Indian manufacturing sector to follow a relatively capital-intensive path, though India has a comparative advantage in labour-intensive technology. The transformation in India's trade pattern from exports of primary goods to finished goods indicates the establishment of production base in India. The production in manufacturing industries is always associated with energy use on the one hand and emissions on the other, the extent of which varies according to the type of manufacturing activity and efficiencies in production. Under imperfect competition, the market is not able to capture these effects: hence, these are referred to as externalities.

There are both positive and negative externalities of the market- and outward-oriented growth processes. The positive externalities arise due to exposure to advanced technologies with the presence of foreign firms. The spillover effect is enjoyed by other firms having low technologies, which further accelerates the growth of domestic output. Furthermore, the market-oriented approach leads to research and innovations and knowledge sharing activities. The negative externalities arise in terms of environmental pollution as well as decrease in the value of environmental resources. Though these negative externalities do not affect the manufacturing process in the short run, but it may have severe effect on the agricultural productivity, human health, and plant and animal lives. Also, the decrease in agricultural productivity aggravates the problem of regional inequality, unemployment, food insecurity, volatility of food prices, etc. When the pollution output coefficient is high, the market economy growth rate exceeds the socially efficient growth rate. This may threaten the sustainability of the growth process.

Looking into India's reforms package of 1991, there was no concern – directly or indirectly – for the environmental quality. Rather, under the zeal of achieving the higher economic growth via export promotion activities and competitive pressures from the outside world, cost-cutting strategy was adopted. Apart from decrease in wages, contractualization, outsourcing, etc., this included bringing down the environmental standards through low-level technologies, zero or minimum abatement cost and weak monitoring mechanism. On the contrary, the developed countries have stricter environmental norms. Strict environmental regulations increase the cost of production as the producers have to spare resources for pollution control measures, or penalties for crossing the emission limits. Owing to this, instead of looking at the comparative advantage in terms of cheap labour, factor endowments, specialization, etc., it could be seen in terms of cross-country differences in environmental laws and regulations. This increases the probability of migration of pollution-intensive industries/technologies to countries with weaker environmental norms (i.e. less developed countries). Furthermore, the FDI is likely to divert to such countries for the production of pollution- or resource-intensive goods. Such countries sometimes experience political lobbying (in the sectors with increased output) or lobbying incentives in other areas of regulation such as environmental policy, with a consequent waste of scarce resources. Presently, environmentally sensitive goods (ESGs) account for approximately one-third of India's merchandise export basket.[9] This implies that trade liberalization does not guarantee specialization in line with a country's comparative advantage if other policies militate against the efficient pattern of resource allocation. Besides, free trade through competitive pressures might compel the developing countries to further reduce their environmental standards.

India has achieved a fairly high growth rate under various strands of liberal policy reforms. The trend growth rate of GDP in the last 20 years has been more than 6 per cent per annum. The growth rate was nearly 9 per cent per annum during 2003–04 to 2007–08 and 9.3 per cent during 2005–08. Manufacturing sector showed a growth rate of 14.3 per cent and 10.3 per cent, respectively, in 2006–07 and 2007–08 (Economic Survey, Various Issues). The country is now a $1.8 trillion economy, the fourth largest in the world (India Development Report 2012–13). On account of its higher growth rate, Indian economy recovered quickly after the 2008–09 crisis period. Growth rate of GDP increased significantly from 6.7 per cent in 2008–09 to 8.4 per cent in 2009–10 in spite of drought. The manufacturing sector's growth rate was 9.7 per cent in 2009–10 as compared to 4.4 per cent in 2007–08. GDP growth was 8.4 per cent in 2010–11 with a growth of 7 per cent and 7.6 per cent in agriculture and manufacturing sector, respectively. India's manufacturing sector currently accounts for about 17 per cent of real (measured) GDP, and close to 80 per cent of merchandise exports, and attract a significant share of FDI. India's exports during the post-reform period have been growing faster than the rate of growth of world exports (COMTRADE-WITS).

The growth–environment model suggests pollution to be a positive function of scale of output up to a certain level of growth. After that the growth itself improves the environmental quality through pollution control measures. Also, the increase in real income increases the demand for environmental quality. Advocates of freer trade suggest that countries that are more open to trade can adopt clean technologies more quickly. Now since India has achieved a sufficient growth rate and a substantial degree of internal and external liberalization during the past two and a half decades, the question arises whether India has reached to that stage of growth, after which the environmental quality increases automatically? For this, there is a need to look into the post-reform changes taking place in the structure and composition of manufacturing activities, FDI, technology and trade pattern. The impact of these changes on environmental externalities, as well as their effect on social well-being, also needs to be explored.

Plenty of literature is available on inter-relationship between income and environmental quality. The issue is highly been explored in developed economies. Few studies have measured the implications of trade for the environment. However, such studies on India are completely lacking. India is a developing economy with its unique characteristics of demographic, geographical, socio-economic and cultural set-up. Besides its growth induced development factors, particularly related to social attitudes and institutions respond in a manner that is different from the other countries. India has a long standing of agricultural economy. With the process of growth, factors are gradually shifting to non-agricultural sector. On account of this, the studies available on trade, growth and environment cannot be treated on the same footing. Rather, there is a need for a country-specific as well as a region-specific approach. Moreover, the impact of pollution is more in the surrounding of the industrial set-up. The severity of this impact varies according to socio-economic set-up of the surrounding. Therefore, in order to articulate the problems of trade-led environmental externalities and its impact on society in a realistic manner, both macro- and micro-level approaches are required.

1.5 Objectives of the Study

The study is based upon the following objectives:

1. To study the growth and composition of Indian manufacturing industries after liberalization.
2. To examine the pollution effects of trade liberalization in terms of scale, composition and technique effects.
3. To determine the causes of growth of dirty industries in India.
4. To find the impact of environmental externalities on the human well-being.

1.6 Hypothesis

1. Trade liberalization has led to increase in production from pollution-intensive industries.
2. Trade liberalization has increased the exports from pollution-intensive industries.
3. Trade liberalization has increased the inflow of intermediates, capital and FDI into pollution-intensive industries.
4. Increase in domestic output shifts the production in favour of clean production process.
5. Environmental externalities affect the quality of life of local people.

1.7 Scope and Coverage

The present study covers the issue of trade liberalization, economic growth and environmental externalities with a focus on Indian manufacturing industries both at the macro and micro levels. At the macro level, the study examines the changes in tariff structure, FDI, technological changes, composition of exports and imports and trade directions over the period of time after the reforms. By comparing the various liberalization measures at industry level, the study tries to identify the importance of various industries from the growth perspective. Since growth nowadays is recognized in terms of trade openness, structural changes in the Indian manufacturing industries are determined in terms of capital–labour ratio, FDI, technological changes and value added per worker in relation to trade openness. All the monetary values in real terms are taken into account.

Further, in order to determine the environmental externalities due to manufacturing activity, pollution loads are calculated on the basis of Industrial Pollution Projection System (IPPS) coefficients developed by World Bank. There is no country-specific method to determine the pollution load, so the trade–environment studies have to depend on IPPS coefficients only. For India, these pollution loads are highly correlated with the pollution intensity measured by Central Pollution Control Board. The rank correlations were used to determine the extent to which the scale of manufacturing output is related with the pollution load. The trade liberalization effects on environmental externalities are determined in terms of scale effect, composition effect and technique effect. The models in linear and non-linear forms enabled us to estimate how the environmental externalities change with the process of growth. The macro-level approach is based upon the secondary sources of data.

Micro-level approach is adopted to determine how the environmental externalities affect the social well-being. Through the field-level study, all the demographic, employment, awareness, experience, education, agricultural productivity- and pollution-related variables were taken into account. The impact of all these variables on social well-being is estimated by ordinal logit model and marginal effects.

On the one hand, the study determines the environmental externality due to trade-led manufacturing growth, and, on the other hand, by investigating the impacts of environmental externality on social well-being, it suggests the measures to minimize the social cost. The study focuses on other growth-related development factors that could be improved to mitigate the risk due to environmental externality. The study, in its true vein explores, the relationship between trade liberalization, economic growth and environmental externality by taking the case of Indian manufacturing industries. In a broader perspective, its results would help the other sectors, regions as well as other developing countries (that are facing similar problems) to frame their policies in order to minimize the social cost of environmental externality. It is hoped that the study would provide valuable insights to the policymakers, planners, administrators and social scientists to deal with the trade induced environmental externalities from a socio-economic perspective.

1.8 Plan of the Study

The book is divided into eight chapters. Chapter 1 gives an overview of trade liberalization, growth and environmental externality, statement of the problem, objectives and scope of the study. Chapter 2 reviews the related existing literature in the global and Indian context. Chapter 3 discusses the methodology adopted for the study. Chapter 4 deals with India's growth experiences of trade liberalization during the past two decades (1991–2011). Chapter 5 observes the structural changes in Indian manufacturing industries due to trade openness. Chapter 6 estimates the environmental externality due to trade induced manufacturing growth. Chapter 7 measures the impact of environmental externality on social well-being on the basis of field survey. Finally, Chapter 8 summarizes and concludes the major findings of the study and points out the policy implications to the policymakers.

Notes

1. Competitiveness implies relative efficiency in producing tradable goods (Mondal and Pant 2014).
2. According to Mani and Wheeler (1997), environmental pricing is the significant determinant of comparative advantage.
3. See Low and Yates (1992), Fredriksson (1999) and Broner et al. (2012).
4. Opportunity cost is measured by the marginal rate of transformation between one good and another, as given by the slope of the production possibility curve; that is, by how much one good has to be sacrificed in order to produce another.
5. Static gains from trade stem from the basic fact that countries are differently endowed with resources (natural and acquired), and because of this the opportunity cost of producing product varies from country to country. In other words, the static gains from trade are measured by the resource gains to be obtained by exporting to obtain imports more cheaply in terms of resources given up, compared to producing the goods oneself. Or, to put it another way, the static gains from trade are measured by the excess cost of import substitution, by what is saved by not producing the imported good domestically. The resource gains can then be used in a variety of ways

including increased domestic consumption of both goods. See Acharyya (2013) for detail.

6. See Helpman and Krugman (1985) for modern trade theory and Grossman and Helpman (1991) for 'New' growth theory.
7. Neoclassical supply-side model (Thirlwal 2000; Feder 1983).
8. See Acharyya (2013), Copeland and Taylor (1994) and Hettige et al. (2000).
9. See Chakraborty (2012).

References

Acharyya, Rajat. (2013): *Trade and Environment*, Oxford University Press, New Delhi.

Bhalla, G.S. (2008): "Globalization and Employment Trends in India", *The Indian Journal of Labour Economics*, Vol. 51(1).

Bhat, T.P. (2013): "Growth and Structural Change in Indian Industry", *Working Paper No. 2013/02*, ISID, New Delhi, February.

Broner, Fernando, Paula Bustos, and Vasco M. Carvalho. (2012): "Sources of Comparative Advantage in Polluting Industries", *NBER Working Paper Series 18337*, NBER, Cambridge, August.

Chakraborty, D. (2012): "Is India Turning into a Pollution Haven? Evidences from Trade and Investment Patterns", in Sacchidananda Mukherjee and Debashis Chakraborty (ed.): *Environmental Scenario in India: Successes and Predicaments*, Routledge, New York.

Copeland, B.R., and M.S. Taylor. (1994): "North-South Trade and the Environment", *The Quarterly Journal of Economics*, Vol. 109(3).

Feder, G. (1983): "On Exports and Economic Growth", *Journal of Development Economics*, Vol. 12(1-2).

Fredriksson, P.G. (1999): "The Political Economy of Trade Liberalization and Environmental Policy", *Southern Economic Journal*, Vol. (3), January.

Grossman, Gene, and Elhanan Helpman. (1991): *Innovation and Growth in the Global Economy*, MIT Press, Cambridge.

Helpman, E., and P. Krugman. (1985): *Market Structure and Foreign Trade: Increasing Returns, Imperfect Competition and the International Economy*, The MIT Press, Cambridge.

Hettige, H.P., M. Mani, and D. Wheeler. (2000): "Industrial Pollution in Economic Development: The Environmental Kuznets Curve Revisited", *Journal of Development Economics*, Vol. 62.

India Development Report, 2012–13, edited by S. Mahendra Dev, Oxford University Press.

Jaffe, Adam B., Steven R. Peterson, Paur R. Portney, and Robert N. Stavins. (1995): "Environmental Regulation and the Competitiveness of U.S. Manufacturing: What Does the Evidence Tell Us?", *Journal of Economic Literature*, Vol. 33(1), March.

Jha, Shrehasi, and Shanti Gamper Rabindran. (2004): "Environmental Impact of India's Trade Liberalization", *https://www.gtap.agecon.purdue.edu/resources/download/1690.pdf*, accessed on 16 October 2014.

Krishna, Pravin, and Devashish Mitra. (1998): "Trade Liberalization, Market Discipline and Productivity Growth: New Evidence from India", *Journal of Development Economics*, Vol. 56(2), 4.

Low, D., and A. Yates. (1992): "Do Dirty Industries Migrate", in P. Low (ed.): *International Trade and Environment*", World Bank, Washington.

Lucas, R.E. (1988): "On the Mechanics of Economic Development", *Journal of Monetary Economics*, Vol. 22.

Mani, Muthukumara, and David Wheeler. (1997): "In Search of Pollution Havens? Dirty Industry in the World Economy, 1960–1999", *World Bank Working Paper No. 16*, April.

Mondal, Sanghita, and Manoj Pant. (2014): "FDI and Firm Competitiveness: Evidence from Indian Manufacturing", *Economic and Political Weekly*, Vol. XLIX, 38, September.

Mukhopadhyay, Kakali, and Debesh Chakraborty. (2005): "Is Liberalization of Trade Good for the Environment? Evidence from India", *Asia Pacific Development Journal*, Vol. 12(1), June.

Nayyar, Deepak. (2011): *Liberalization and Development*, Oxford University Press, Delhi.

Neher, Philip A. (1990): *Natural Resource Economics: Conservation and Exploitation*, Cambridge University Press, New York.

Ogunrinola, I. (2013): "How Far and Wide? A Cointegration Analysis of Trade Openness and Economic Growth in Nigeria (1980-2011)", *Journal of Business Administration and Management Sciences Research*, Vol. 2(12), December.

Panayotou, T. (1993): "Empirical Tests and Policy Analysis of Environmental Degradation at Different Stages of Economic Development", *Working Paper 238*, Technology and Employment Programme, Geneva, International Labour Office.

Rajakumar, J.Dennis. (2011): "Size and Growth of Private Corporate Sector in Indian Manufacturing", *Economic and Political Weekly*, Vol. 46(18).

Romer, P. (1986): "Increasing Returns and Long-run Growth", *Journal of Political Economy*, Vol. 94.

Smith, Adam. (1776): *An Inquiry into the Nature and Causes of the Wealth of Nations.*

Stokey, N. (1988): "Learning by Doing and the Introduction of New Goods", *Journal of Political Economy*, Vol. 96.

Thirlwall, Anthony P. (2000): "Trade, Trade Liberalization and Economic Growth Theory and Evidence", *Economic Research Papers No. 63*, The African Development Bank, Abidijan.

WTO. (2004): *Trade and Environment at the WTO: Background Document*, WTO, Geneva.

CHAPTER 2

Review of the Existing Literature

Abstract The issue of economic growth and environmental quality has largely been discussed by various social scientists, economic thinkers and environmentalists. The relationship of trade and environment has also received considerable attention. This chapter presents the review of the existing studies under (i) trade liberalization-led economic growth; (ii) liberalized policies (on trade and investment) and its environmental implications at global and India levels; (iii) growth–environment interactions; (iv) market economy, property rights and environmental externalities. However, the studies measuring the impact of economic reforms on environment are scant at India level. Since the nature of externalities and its impact on society depends upon various socio-economic factors, such studies require a country-/area-specific approach.

Keywords Trade · Environment · Market economy · Externalities

The economic reforms of 1991 attracted the attention of various social scientists, researchers and policymakers. Particularly, the relationship of economic growth with openness to foreign trade in goods and services, technology and investment has attracted a good deal of theoretical and empirical attention. Since the liberal trade policy regimes transforms the production process on the basis of comparative advantage, the environmental implications of trade liberalization has also gained importance.

H. Jain, *Trade Liberalisation, Economic Growth and Environmental Externalities*, DOI 10.1007/978-981-10-2887-8_2

Previously, the issue of environmental quality was confined to the developed countries only. Since the manufacturing activity[1] has environmental consequences at both the local and global levels, this has influenced the researchers and the policymakers to drive their attention towards environmental externalities due to trade-oriented manufacturing growth in both developed and developing economies.

This chapter presents a review of the existing studies on trade liberalization, economic growth and environmental externalities under five sections. Section 2.1 reviews the studies on trade liberalization-led economic growth. Section 2.2 presents a review of the studies on liberalized policies (on trade and investment) and its environmental implications at both global and India levels. Section 2.3 deals with the studies on growth–environment interactions. Section 2.4 covers the studies on market economy, property rights and environmental externalities. Finally section 2.5 concludes the chapter.

2.1 Studies on Trade Liberalization-Led Economic Growth

Several studies have accepted that the growth effects of open trade policies apparently arise from an acceleration of investment and an increase in the rate of adoption of new technologies that an export-oriented strategy seems to bring about (Lopez 1994; Mani and Wheeler 1997; Dietzenbacher and Mukhopadhyay 2007; Mani and Jha 2006; Balassa 1982; Kavossi 1984; Ram 1985). Focusing on the post-reform growth of Indian economy, Hirway and Shah (2011) showed that GDP in India has been achieved by adopting highly capital-intensive technology, and the higher the jump an economy has taken in terms of technology, the higher the growth it has achieved. Some of the recent studies like Bhattacharya and Mitra (1993), Agarwal and Goldar (1995), Kundu (1997) and Deshpande et al. (2004) realized that increased competition in a globalized framework is forcing the firms to shift towards more capital-intensive 'advanced technology'. The studies have confirmed a positive correlation between growth of national income and technological change due to liberalization. Papola (2013) has postulated economic growth to be a function of capital investment and incremental capital–output ratio. Mukhopadhyay (2006) has experienced a similar move towards capital-intensive industry than labour-intensive industry in Thai economy during the latter half of the 1990s because of shifting of trade towards more emerging industries. This diversification of trade is supported and encouraged by the foreign capital to few related export sectors. The authors explained that to be competitive in the global market, the production units have adopted the latest frontier technologies, which are usually capital intensive in nature. Also, the increased flow of FDI has brought highly capital-intensive technologies prevailing in the countries from where the funds come. The studies by Babu (2009) and Dokadia and Pellissery (2007) remarked that liberalization of the external sector associated with greater role of the private sector in industrial economy has induced greater competition among national players and between national players and international players. Such a competition has initiated the need to be more productive, with the aim to generate profit, if a firm has to sustain its business. Thus, firms are seeking various ways of reducing cost, increasing efficiency and still remain profitable.

Owing to this, the structure of industrial production has undergone significant changes. According to Unni and Scaria (2009), globalization has led to large-scale outsourcing of production activities to developing countries manifesting in global commodity chains. Chandrasekhar (2011) found that the factor influencing manufacturing growth during the post-liberalization years was the increase in access to domestically assembled or produced import-intensive manufactured goods. Mukhopadhyay (2006) observed the similar trend for Thailand, where import from OECD (Organisation for Economic Co-operation and Development) comprises raw materials, machinery and equipment necessary to fuel the exports of manufacturing sector. In this context Hirway and Shah (2011) highlighted the fact that global market, dominated by global production network, is under the control of multinational corporations (MNCs), which keep core activities such as sale, design and finance with themselves while distributing production process among developing countries. These countries are forced to globalize at the lowest end of the value chain by cutting their all types of production costs so as to survive cut-throat competition and acquired order from MNCs. Thus trade-oriented economic growth is based on measuring the manufacturing profit by minimizing the cost to the possible extent.

2.2 Studies Related to Liberalized Policies and Its Environmental Implications

2.2.1 *Global Scenario*

2.2.1.1 Trade Liberalization and Environmental Implications

Several studies have addressed different aspects of trade liberalization policies and its implications for the environment. The advocates of free trade suggest that the more open the economy, the less pollution intensive it is (Birdsall and Wheeler 1993). While the critics of free trade argued that the more open the economy, the more pollution intensive it is (Rock 1996). Taking into consideration the existence of environmental regulation gaps between developed and developing countries, the studies have considered that free trade is bad for the environment in developing countries (Grether et al. 2007). This is confirmed by Low and Yates (1992) and Levinson and Taylor (2001). These studies have found that the export share of polluting goods from industrialized countries to developing countries tended to decrease over time, while the import of dirty goods to the United States (US) increased over the last three decades. While comparing the trade-related pollution impacts in developing and developed countries, Mani and Wheeler (1997) asserted that pollution-intensive output as a percentage of total manufacturing has fallen consistently in the OECD and risen steadily in the developing world. Moreover, the period of rapid increase in net export of pollution-intensive products from developing countries coincided with period of rapid increase in the cost of pollution abatement in the OECD countries. Mani (1996) observed increasing manufacturing and export activity in water and toxic pollution-intensive sectors compared to less pollution-intensive sectors. The author finds the changing composition of Vietnam production and exports away from traditional sectors and towards pollution-intensive manufacturing (especially leather and textile).

On the contrary, Birdsall and Wheeler (1993) from case studies and econometric evidence concluded that protected economies are more likely to favour pollution-intensive industries while openness actually encourages cleaner industries through the importation of developed country's pollution standards. Gallagher (2004) related the trade liberalization and industrial pollution in Mexico and finds that many of the industries deemed to be dirtier in world economy are actually cleaner in Mexico than in the US, and industries labelled the cleanest are dirtier in Mexico. This exhibits that trade liberalization can have both positive and negative environmental effects in developing economies. The author suggests that the sectors where plant vintage determines pollution level can benefit from their ability to take advantage of newer technologies after liberalizing trade. Dean (2002) uses provincial-level data on water pollution from China and found support for the idea that trade liberalization has both a direct and an indirect effect on emission growth and these could be opposite in sign.

Wadeskog (2002) and Lange and Hasan (2002) addressed the issues on trade and environment using input–output (I-O) techniques.[2] The studies were concerned about the impact of foreign trade on local and global environment. Through goods and services traded in a globally interdependent world, consumption in each region is linked to greenhouse gas emission in other regions. The studies are based on the assumption that commodities imported from foreign countries are produced using domestic production technology and energy inputs. The study was further extended by Munksgaard and Pedersen (2001) and Lenzen (2001) to calculate the amount of energy and greenhouse gases embodied in a value unit of commodities produced by Danish final consumption. Wyckoff and Roop (1994) estimated that a significant amount (about 13 per cent) of the total carbon emission of the six largest OECD countries is embodied in manufactured import. Machado et al. (2001) applied I-O techniques to the Brazilian economy to calculate the total impact of international trade on its energy used and CO_2 emissions. Results show that in 1995, in Brazil, carbon embodied in the exports of non-energy goods were larger than the relevant amount embodied in the imports of non-energy goods. Haan (2002) has derived environmental balance of trade by analysing the trade relationships for a number of trade patterns of the Netherlands. These bilateral environmental balances of trade are further analysed by tracking down differences in the absolute levels of export and import and eco efficiencies (pollution or natural resource requirement per unit of product). The cross-country studies like Gerilla et al. (2002) for China and Japan, Przybylinski (2002) for Poland and Germany, Hayami and Nakamura (2002) for Japan and Canada and Ahmed (2002) for selected OECD countries are worth mentioning in this respect.

The studies have also related the trade-induced environmental pollution with factor intensity and relative factor prices. According to Antweiler et al. (2001) and Cole and Elliott (2001), pollution-intensive goods are relatively capital intensive. Mani and Wheeler (1997) submit that dirty industries are relatively intensive in capital, energy and land; their clean counterparts are relatively intensive in labour. Grossman and Kruger (1993) estimated factor prices and tariffs to be important determinants for trade and investment pattern in Mexico and US. In the same context, Cole et al. (2001) tested a monopolistic competition model of inter-industry and intra-industry trade to examine the North–South trade patterns. They submitted that the role played by foreign trade seems to be highly significant in affecting the use of natural resources (energy induced) and in generating environmental damage in countries in particular, as well as in the world as a whole. Hirway and Shah (2011) opined that rapid industrial growth is usually achieved through destruction of natural resources (i.e. overusing natural resources without adequate replenishment) and pollution of air, water and land (in the absence of proper regulation). Boyd et al. (1993) and Cruz and Repetto (1993) have claimed that removal of trade barriers as a part of trade liberalization have resulted into increased deforestation in Philippines. Stern (2002) claimed that manufacturing emissions account for approximately one-third of global anthropogenic SO_2 emissions, the rest being roughly split in half between power generation and other activities.[3]

2.2.1.2 Financial Liberalization, Environmental Standards and Industrial Relocation

In the realm of liberal trade policies, the countries take into consideration their comparative advantage in international trade taking into account the differences in enactment of environmental laws and establishment of regulatory agencies by developed and developing countries. Stricter regulation means polluter pay more for pollution equipment, conversion to cleaner process, or penalties for unacceptable emissions. Mani and Wheeler (1997) argue that this regulatory gap between developed and developing countries could in principle, produce 'pollution havens' analogous to 'low-wage havens'. However, there are different views in this regard. Xing and Kolstad (1997), Low and Yates (1992) and Fredriksson (1999) submitted that the dirty industries relocate to countries with lax environmental regulation. According to Grether et al. (2007), the conjunction of differences in environmental policies and in the determinants of trade across countries may lead the migration of 'dirty' industries to the countries with emission-intensive production techniques. Hettige et al. (1992) observed the similar phenomenon of 'industrial displacement effect' for the dirtier industries as a result of the tightening of environmental regulations in the industrialized countries since 1970. For Xing and Kolstad (1997), laxity of environmental regulations in a host country is a significant determinant of FDI for polluting industries. Smarzynska and Wei (2004) used firm-level data on investment projects in 24 transition economies and found some support for the pollution haven hypothesis (PHH). Cole et al. (2008) found the similar results for China. In a similar sense, Levinson and Taylor (2001) used a 2SLS (two-stage least squares) procedure with instruments to measure stringency of environmental regulations across states in the US, to capture the endogenous nature of the trade–environment relationship. Using this method, they found that tighter environmental regulations are associated with larger net imports. Eskeland and Harrison (2003) also examined PHH using data on US FDIs whether multinationals tend to flock to pollution havens in developing countries. Gamper-Rabindran and Jha (2004) in the post-1991 analysis of FDI inflows revealed that foreign investment were higher in industries that are more intensive in air and water pollution.

Focusing on Southeast Asian economies, Mukhopadhyay (2006) reported adverse environmental implications of FDI flows from OECD countries to Thailand. Merican et al. (2007) also observed that FDI inflows add to pollution quotient in Malaysia, Thailand and Philippines. CUTS (2003) noted that countries like Papua New Guinea, the Philippines and Indonesia had lowered their environmental standard to attract FDI inflow in mining sector. Jaffe et al. (1993) in his study on majority-owned affiliates of the OECD-based companies in developing countries pointed out that those involved in pollution-intensive industries did increase their investment slightly faster than did all manufacturing industries. Focusing on outward FDI flows of various industries within German manufacturing sector, Wagner and Timmins (2008) showed robust evidence of PHH for the chemical industry. Aminu (2005) demonstrated that 'dirty' FDI outflow is positively correlated with environmental policy in eleven OECD countries.

In contrast, some studies refuted the existence of pollution havens in developing countries having lax environmental standards (Mani and Wheeler 1999; Rock 2002; Grossman and Krueger 1993). Dean et al. (2004) argued that while weaker environmental levies act as significant attraction for Chinese joint ventures (JVs) with partners from Southeast

Asian developing countries, JVs from industrial countries (e.g. US, United Kingdom (UK) and Japan) are attracted by stronger environmental levies, regardless of the pollution intensity of the industry. Grossman and Krueger (1993) examined environmental impact of NAFTA and found no evidence that a comparative advantage is being created by lax environmental regulations in Mexico. Mani and Wheeler suggests that pollution-intensive industries (i.e. those with low elasticities of substitution between use of the environment and other productive factors) might join labour-intensive industries in the migration from the OECD countries to open developing economies, if the latter remained unregulated and environmental pricing were a significant determinant of comparative advantage. Eskeland and Harrison (1997) examined industry-level FDI in four developing countries (Mexico, Cote d' Ivoire, Venezuela and Morocco) and found no significant positive correlation between industry-level FDI and measures of air and water emissions. Copeland and Taylor (2003a) in their study on SO_2 emissions concluded that 'free trade is good for the environment'. The study suggests that free trade will shift pollution-intensive goods production from poor countries with lax regulation to rich countries with tight regulation, thereby lowering world pollution. Antweiler et al. (2001) also considered the relocation of pollution-intensive industries production from countries in the labour-abundant South to those in the relatively capital-abundant North. According to Copeland and Taylor (2003b), the environmental policy differences combined with factor endowments explains the heterogeneity across the industries as well as countries. Tobey (1990) tested the international trade pattern of five polluting industries for 23 countries and Cole et al. (2001) selected four trading partners, viz. UK–Asia, US–Asia, US–Latin America and Japan–Asia. Both studies have found no statistical significance of environmental regulation measures on the net export as well as on existence of PHH and factor endowment hypothesis (FEH). Prakash and Potoski (2006) claimed that factors like capital abundance, technology differences, infrastructure, etc. are far more important as compared to environmental policy in determining trade and FDI patterns. FDI is also argued to bring best environmental practices and adoption of cleaner norms. The theoretical model by Das and Das (2007) has also questioned the existence of PHH.

It is interesting to note here that even the environmental policy determination is influenced by changes in trade policy regime. Husted and Logsdon (1997) reported that the North American Free Trade

Agreement (NAFTA) has induced Mexico to strengthen its environmental policies. In simulations by Perroni and Wigle (1994), trade policy is found to have little impact on the quality of environment, given the level of environmental regulation. However, they found that global increase of pollution taxes to the optimal levels would improve environmental quality significantly. Fredriksson (1999) estimated the effects of trade liberalization on the special interest groups' lobbying incentives on the pollution tax issue. Ceteris Paribus, when output contracts in the polluting sector following trade liberalization, both lobby groups reduce their lobbying on the tax issue in the new equilibrium because the marginal return to a change in the tax decreases. If the pollution tax falls (increases) sufficiently as a result of trade liberalization, pollution increases (decreases) through the pollution channels.

2.2.2 Indian Scenario

The post-reforms studies on India notes adverse environmental performance by transnational corporations during the 1980s (Jha 1999) and higher FDI inflow in relatively more polluting sectors (Singh 1997; Gamper-Rabindran and Jha 2004). Mathys (2004) attempted to explain this trend by arguing that globalization of Indian economy has been associated with increased activities in polluting products. Chattopadhyay (2005) has also noted an increase in India's export of polluting products.

Jha and Rabindran (2004) found that the share of polluting industries in total manufacturing sector has been increasing in the post-liberalization era in comparison to the pre-liberalization period. The study also reveals that both FDI and export have grown in the more polluting sectors (specifically water- and air-pollution-intensive industries) relative to the less polluting sectors in the post-liberalization period. After controlling for potential intervening variables and correcting for sample selection bias, the authors find that the post-1991 coefficients on air and water pollution intensity are positive (0.01 and 0.80, respectively). The results on FDI and net exports are robust to different empirical specifications.

Taking the case of an individual manufacturing unit, Tewari (2000) examined how the automobile and leather industries in the state of Tamil Nadu in India are coping up with new environmental challenges in the post-liberalization period. Gupta (2000) also examined the impact of

India's trade and investment liberalization on the environment by assembling industry-level economic and environmental data across India.

However, several studies have rejected the existence of pollution haven phenomenon in India (Mukhopadhyay 2004; Jena et al. 2005; Mukhopadhyay and Chakraborty 2005b; Dietzenbacher and Mukhopadhyay 2007). Mukhopadhyay and Chakraborty (2004) tested two hypothesis: PHH and FEH during the 1990s. Using I-O method, they found that import-related pollution is much larger than the export-related pollution for India. The authors submitted that their findings challenge the PHH arguing that liberalization of trade policy in India has not been associated with pollution-intensive industrial development. But, it supports the FEH thus confirming that the export-oriented labour requirement are much more in weight than its import counterpart. Hence India gains in terms of emission from trade in both cases.

Mukhopadhyay and Chakraborty (2005a) estimated India's environmental gains or losses from trade with other countries. The results reveal that India does not suffer from pollution haven as its pollution terms of trade is found to be below 100. But it does support the factor endowments by exporting labour-intensive goods which are environmental friendly. It was concluded that trade may lead both a cleaner environment in poor countries and a reduction in global pollution. The results point out that differences in pollution policy alone need not imply that trade liberalization will force dirty industries to migrate to less regulated countries. Jena et al. (2005) by considering a pooled cross-section model on a sample of 17 states for the period 1991–2002, estimated for air pollution variables such as sulphur dioxide (SO_2), nitrogen oxide (NO_x) and suspended particulate matters (SPM). The estimated results reveal that foreign investment has played a very negligible role in the concentration of air pollutants whereas; regional economic growth is found to have caused the accumulation of environmental problems.

Chakraborty (2012) argued that the presence of FDI in polluting sectors in India is more of a sector-specific phenomenon rather than region-specific. Mukherjee and Chakraborty (2009) show that with rise in income, and consequently in human development, the States get relatively 'cleaner'. Hence the direct linkage between IEM and pollution gets weakened. However, the relationship between implemented IEM and emission level is confirmed in the case of SO_2.

2.3 Studies on Growth–Environment Nexus

Regarding the growth–environment relationship, there are two extremes. At one extreme, growing economic activity (production and consumption) requires larger inputs of energy and material, and generates larger quantities of waste by-products (Georgescu 1971; Meadows et al. 1972). Increased extraction of natural resources, accumulation of waste and concentration of pollution will therefore overwhelm the carrying capacity of biosphere and result in degradation of the environmental quality and a decline in human welfare, despite rising incomes (Daly 1991). At the other extreme, the fastest road to environmental improvement is along the path of economic growth; higher income increases demand for goods and services that are less material intensive, as well as demand for improved environmental quality that leads to adoption of environmental protection measures (Panayotou 1997). Some authors focus on shifts in production technology brought about by structural changes accompanying economic growth (Grossman and Krueger 1995), others have emphasized on abatement technology (Andreoni and Levinson 2000) and yet others have focused on preferences, especially the income elasticity for environmental quality (McConnell 1997). Dasgupta et al. (1995), Mukhopadhyay and Chakraborty (2005a, b), Cole and Rayner (2000), Copeland and Taylor (2003a, b), Anderson (1993) and so on have tried to determine the correlation between economic growth and environmental pollution. Dasgupta et al. (1995) document that the stringency of environmental regulation increases with income and economic development. According to Mukhopadhyay and Chakraborty (2005b), rich countries have a higher willingness to pay for environmental quality and thus set higher environmental standards. The cross-sectional studies by the World Bank suggests that some environmental problems, such as water pollution and sanitation, are most severe at low-income levels, while others, such as emission of greenhouse gases, are worst in high-income countries (World Bank 1992). Perhaps, air pollution (SO_2, SPM, and other pollutants) seem to be worst in middle-income countries (Grossman and Krueger 1991).[4]

Focusing on the income gains and sectoral production changes induced by Uruguay Round and on several air pollutants (including SO_2), Cole and Rayner (2000) used the IPPS database. They find that the Uruguay Round would decrease SO_2 emissions in European Union and the US and that emissions would rise for developing and transition economies. Mani and Wheeler (1998) stated that tendencies towards formation of pollution havens in developing countries are self-limiting, because economic growth generates countervailing effects through increase in regulation, technical expertise and investment in cleaner production. Pollution intensity has an elastic response to income growth. The authors estimated that if the income elasticity of regulation is greater than one, then developing countries will not retain a comparative advantage in dirty production. As a result, the developing countries will move closer to locally appropriate level of pollution control. The author is hopeful that as the developing economies prosper and tighten their regulations, the shadow of pollution levels will recede to insignificance. Lopez (1994) discussed that economic growth increases the value of environment for consumers. If this increased value is manifested in the market, firms will have to pay an increasing price for pollution. A higher elasticity of substitution in production between conventional inputs and pollution implies that firms need to spend less conventional inputs to reduce pollution in response to a higher pollution price.

Copeland and Taylor (2003a) have shown an indirect relationship between economic growth and pollution. The study reveals that pollution declines amid economic growth fuelled by economy-wide technological progress but rises when growth is fuelled by capital accumulation. Antweiler et al. (2001) observed that income gains brought about by further trade or neutral technological progress tend to lower pollution, while income gains brought about by capital accumulation raise pollution. The key difference is that capital accumulation necessarily favours the production of pollution-intensive goods, whereas neutral technological progress and further trade do not. The study claims that the pollution consequences of economic growth are dependent on the underlying sources of growth. Income effect appears to be economically and statistically significant, and the trade-induced composition effects are not driven by differences in pollution regulations. Alongwith income growth, Lantz and Feng (2006) and Galeotti and Lanza (1999) found population growth to have a positive effect on CO_2 emissions. Lopez (1994) considered the effect of factor expansion on pollution to depend on two critical parameters: the elasticity of substitution in production between pollution and non-pollution inputs, and the relative degree of curvature of the utility function in income. The smaller the technical substitution possibilities between pollution and non-pollution input and the smaller the 'degree of relative risk aversion', the more likely is that pollution will increase with growth even if preferences are non-homothetic.

While explaining the income–environment relationship, a number of studies have confirmed the existence of Environment Kuznets Curve (EKC) hypothesis (Stern 2004, 2005; Olivier and Berdowski 2001; Grossman and Krueger 1993). The studies accepted that many environmental characteristics first deteriorate and then eventually improve once a sufficiently high-income level is reached, thus following an inverted 'U' trend for various pollutants. Kristrom (2000) suggests that the exact shape of the relationship and the turning point, if any, depend on the interplay of the technology and preference parameter, which differ among pollutants and circumstances. While few have questioned its existence (Bruyn et al. 1998; Aslanidis and Iranzo 2009; Narayan and Narayan 2010; Pauli 2003). Cole et al. (1997) found inverted U-shaped curves only for local air pollutants and chlorofluorocarbons (CFCs), while indication with a more global, more indirect, environmental impact either increase with income or have high turning points with large standard errors. According to Panayotou and Islam (1999) and Panayotou and Vincent (1997), the scale effect on pollution, controlling for the other two effects, is expected to be monotonically increasing function of income while the composition effect is likely to be a non-monotonic (inverted U) function of GDP. Panayotou (2000) accepted that the income variable (stripped of its scale and composition effects) captures the locus of equilibrium abatement levels, where demand and supply, both income-dependent, are equal. Hence, abatement effect is expected to be a monotonically decreasing function of income. Cole (2003) suggested that emissions are monotonic in income and reductions in emissions are time related rather than income related. It is a change either in output composition, or, most likely, in emission per unit of output that would account for the reversal in emission trends rather than income changes as postulated in the EKC theory. According to Bruyn et al. (1998), emissions may decline over time, probably due to technological and structural changes. In the words of Panayotou (1997), the turning point of EKC and its height is largely determined by market efficiency and policy interventions and partly by income level. Munasinghe (1995) recommends an adjustment of timing and sequencing of policy reforms and complementary measures to address specific distortions and 'tunnel through' the EKC, while cautioning against the temptation of making major changes in economy-wide policies merely to achieve minor environmental (and social) gains.

Studies such as Strutt and Anderson (1998), Antweiler et al. (2001), Dean (2002) and Gupta (2002) consider that the trade policy reforms would improve the environment (at least with respect to air and water pollution) and reduce the depletion of natural resources, and in the worst cases add only slightly to environmental degradation and resource depletion even without toughening the enforcement of environmental regulation or adding new ones. John and Pecchennino (1994) suggest that multiple Pareto-ranked equilibria can arise as a result of the interaction between capital accumulation and environmental quality. When the economy is dynamically efficient in terms of capital and environment, Pareto improvements can be implemented by a long-lived planner. These studies are hopeful that economic gains from trade reforms and the scope for adopting well-targeted environmental resource policies to reduce any serious damage are such that the social welfare almost certainly is going to be improved substantially by these liberalizations (Jena et al. 2005).

In some of the studies, the impact of trade on environment is determined by decomposing the emission changes into scale, composition and technique effects. The relevant studies have considered an interplay between these three effects, however, the forces of interplay varies. Grether et al. (2007) estimated the impact of trade on worldwide SO_2 emission over the period 1990–2000. Combining three emission data sources (Industrial Pollution Projection System, Electronic Data Gathering, Analysis and Retrieval System and Stern (2006)) with sectoral output and employment data, they constructed a database with time-, country- and sector-specific emission coefficients. A first-growth decomposition exercise show that scale and technique effect are the main driving force behind global changes in SO_2 emissions. A second exercise compares the actual trade situation with an autarky benchmark. It shows that trade, by allowing clean countries to become net importers of emissions, leads to a roughly 10 per cent increase in world emissions with respect to autarky in 1990, but this figure shrinks to 3.5 per cent in 2000. This decrease in the effect is consistent with the negative composition effects found in the first exercise. A third exercise uses linear programming to stimulate extreme situation where world emissions are either maximal or minimal. It turns out that effective emissions correspond to a 90 per cent reduction with respect to the worst case, but that another 80 per cent reduction would be reached if emissions were minimal.

Antweiler et al. (2001) also used data on SO_2 concentration from the Global Environment Monitoring project. They estimated that international trade creates relatively small changes in pollutant concentrations when it alters the composition, and hence the pollution intensity, of national output. Their estimates of the associated technique and scale effects created by trade imply a net reduction in pollution from these sources. Combining the estimates of scale, composition and technique effects, the author finds that if trade liberalization raises GDP per person by 1 per cent, then pollution concentration falls by about 1 per cent. A 1 per cent increase in scale of economic activity raises pollution concentration by 0.25 per cent to 0.5 per cent for an average country by the accompanying increase in income drives concentrations down by 1.25 to −1.5 per cent. The study finally suggests that the composition effect of trade for poor countries makes them dirtier while the composition effect for rich countries makes them cleaner. The full effect of trade may be positive even for poor countries depending on the strength of the technique or scale effects.

Stern (2002) adopted the decomposition approach for SO_2 emission and finds that scale and technique effects are the dominant forces and that they tend to offset each other. The composition effects (input and output compositions) may, however, be large for a particular country. Using the same theoretical framework but applied to national energy use in 32 countries, Cole (2006) obtains opposite results, namely that the scale effect outweighs the technique effect and that the trade-induced composition effect is positive. Edrington et al. (2004) accepted that trade liberalization can affect the environment via several mechanisms: interjurisdictional competition to lower standards, transfer of pollution abatement technology, cross-border spillovers, changes to the overall scale of economies, etc. But the most direct effect of trade liberalization on the environment would be through composition of industries. Trade liberalization leads to specialization, increasing the concentration of polluting industries in some countries and decreasing it in others. Countries that specialize in less pollution-intensive goods will have cleaner environment. Using annual industry-level data on imports to the US, the authors have estimated a large shift towards cleaner industries. However, the authors find no evidence that pollution-intensive industries have been disproportionately sensitive by the tariff changes over that time period.

2.4 Studies on Market Economy, Property Rights and Environmental Externalities

The gains from trade liberalization depend upon the embodied comparative advantage. Due to the differences in environmental regulations in the countries, apart from the relative prices of factors of production, the comparative advantage for trade could be seen in terms of lax environmental standards (Mani and Wheeler 1999; Fredriksson 1999). The idea of comparative advantage no longer holds if the markets are imperfect (Sanyal 2013). In the presence of market power, price exceeds cost and the difference accrues to the producer as rent. When environmental values are concerned, there are likely to be very substantial differences between market values and social values (Bhattacharya 2013; Greiner 2005; Barro 1990). Chakrobarty (2013) discussed the environmental externalities due to ill-defined property rights. Due to inappropriate ownership of environmental resources (e.g. atmosphere, high seas or the watershed commons), privately perceived rate of return from environmental protection becomes less than the return from activities causing environmental degradation. Panayotou (2000) shows that where markets are riddled with failures (externalities, ill-defined property rights, etc.) or distorted subsidies of environmentally destructive inputs, outputs and processes, the environmental price of economic growth is likely to be significantly higher than otherwise. In Maler's model,[5] the existence of property rights allows environmental resources to be efficiently priced even though agents are short-lived.

Lopez (1994) emphasized that the impact of economic growth and trade policy on environment are usually dependent on the internalization of temporal and inter-temporal environmental externalities by individual producers in the case where productive stock feedback effects are present. The internalization may be induced by private ownership, contractual community arrangements or government policies.

Panayotou (2000) determined that on the supply side, higher income makes available the resources needed for increased private and public expenditures on pollution abatement, and induce stricter environmental regulation that internalize pollution externalities. Arrow et al. (1995) agree for a better understanding of ecosystem dynamics and recommended reforms to improve the signals received by economic agents, including better-defined property rights and institutions that 'provide the right incentives for protecting the resilience of ecological systems'.

2.5 Conclusion

With the policy of liberalization and globalization, the pattern of trade and investment flows among the developed and developing countries has changed. The change has also occurred in the composition of manufactured goods and technologies adopted at the domestic front. The integration with the world economies with reduction in trade barriers has enabled the developing countries to produce more for exports by adopting advanced technologies. The literature review confirmed that at the time of reforms, the developed countries were already having stringent environmental standards as compared to developing countries. Thus finding the impact of trade liberalization on environment in both developed and developing countries became the area of research interest. The studies have worked on different variables, like reduction in trade barriers, FDI inflows, factor endowment, technological changes, industrial relocation, scale, composition and technology effects of manufacturing output, differences in environmental regulation, trade patterns, distribution of world's income, economic growth, property rights, and so on, to find the environmental consequences of increased openness. Some of the studies have separately addressed the air pollutants (SO_2 and CO_2 emission) and water pollutants taking into account their local and global environmental impacts. However, the issue is still debatable. The results of these studies particularly for developing countries vary significantly. Some studies have claimed that due to trade liberalization, the developing countries have become pollution havens for which the others have totally disagreed. Some have accepted the impact to be of moderate level which will diminish with time or can be controlled by framing appropriate environmental policies.

There is sizable literature on India's post-liberalized economic growth focusing on various economic sectors. India's remarkable economic growth during the past decade has attracted researchers from all over the world to find the impact of economic reforms as well as the impact of each measure of reforms on economic growth and related issues. Unfortunately, the studies measuring impact of economic reforms on the environment is scant. Most of them are descriptive and are not able to find the quantum of effect of trade-induced growth on environment. Thus the picture on this issue is very unclear.

After the economic reforms, a spate of changes has occurred in Indian economy. The existing literature considers that an economic prosperity tightens the environmental regulation and makes the pollution haven insignificant. Sometimes the changes in output composition and technological or structural changes themselves reverse the emission trends without toughening the enforcement of environmental regulation. This mobilizes us to explore whether India is following the general phenomenon of trade–environment relationship or the pattern of economic growth achieved during the post-reforms period has brought some remarkable difference. In other words, to what extent the India's recent economic growth has been able to influence environmental externalities?

It is true that openness to trade and investment alters the composition of national output. It is to be noted here that this alteration depends upon the nation's comparative advantage which cannot be similar for all the developing countries. On this basis, considering trade–environment relationship for all the developing countries on the same footing is unlikely to be fruitful. The results obtained on this basis may be highly misleading for framing a country's policy for environmental protection. Instead one should look at the trade's effect on environment by conditioning on country's characteristics (e.g. quality of work force and infrastructure and communication facilities.) that improves with economic growth. Also, as the economy grows, the substitution between income and environmental factor varies. Thus there is a need to determine the current scenario of this substitution.

This study is an attempt to fill this gap by linking the trade-induced economic growth with environmental externalities, taking into account the existing characteristics of Indian economy. The focus is on the manufacturing industries that have shown a high performance in terms of output, export and investment inflows during the post-reforms period. Further, a region-specific approach (on Gujarat) provides a deeper insight into the impact of environmental externality on social well-being. By incorporating the socio-economic variables in the model, the study tries to find the extent to which the growth led other development activities helps to decrease the severity of the impact of environmental externality.

Notes

1. Manufacturing for export has increased the share of developing economies in the world trade.
2. Previously used by Wright (1974), Fieleke (1975), Antweiler (1996) and Proops et al. (1999), for estimating the trade–environment relationship.

3. See Olivier and Berdowski (2001).
4. See John and Pecchennino (1994).
5. See Maler (1993).

References

Agarwal, R.N., and B. Goldar. (1995): "Economic Reforms and Employment in India: Projections for the Year 2001–02", *Indian Journal of Labour Economics*, Vol. 38(4).

Ahmed, N. (2002): "Environmental Spillovers: Energy Use and Carbon Leakages in the OECD, *Paper Presented at the 14th International Conference on Input-Output held at UQAM*, Montreal, Canada, 10–15 October.

Aminu, A.M. (2005): "Foreign Direct Investment and the Environment: Pollution Haven Hypothesis Revisited", *Paper Prepared for the Eight Annual Conference on Global Economic Analysis*, Lübeck, Germany, 9–11 June.

Anderson, K. (1993): "Economic Growth, Environmental Issues and Trade", Centre for Economic Policy and Research, *Discussion Paper No. 830*, London.

Andreoni, James, and Arik Levinson. (2000): "The Simple Analytics of the Environmental Kuznets Curve", *Journal of Public Economics*, Vol. 80.

Antweiler, W. (1996): "The Pollution Terms of Trade", *Economic Systems Research*, Vol. 8(4).

Antweiler, W., B.R. Copeland, and M.S. Taylor. (2001): "Is Free Trade Good for the Environment?", *American Economic Review*, Vol. 91(4).

Arrow, K.J., B. Bolin, R. Costanza, P. Dasgupta, C. Folke, C.S. Ho, B.O. Jansson, S. Levin, K.G. Maler, C. Perrings, and D. Pimendel. (1995): "Economic Growth Carrying Capacity and the Environment", *Science*, 268.

Aslanidis, N., and S. Iranzo. (2009): "Environment and Development: Is There a Kuznets Curve for CO_2 Emissions?", *Applied Economics*, Vol. 41.

Babu, M. Suresh. (2009): "Losing Out in a Growing Economy: Labour in the Organized Manufacturing Sector in the Era of Globalization", *The Indian Journal of Labour Economics*, Vol. 52(2).

Balassa, B. (1982): "Development Strategies and Economic Performance", in B. Balassa (ed.): *Development Strategies in Semi Industrialized Economies*, Oxford University Press, London.

Barro, R.J. (1990): "Government Spending in a Simple Model of Endogenous Growth", *Journal of Political Economy*, Vol. 98.

Bhattacharya, B.B., and A. Mitra. (1993): "Employment and Structural Adjustment: A Look at 1991 Census Data", *Economic and Political Weekly*, September 18.

Bhattacharya, N.R. (2013): *Environmental Economics: An Indian Perspective*, Oxford University Press.

Birdsall, Nancy, and David Wheeler. (1993): "Trade Policy and Industrial Pollution in Latin America: Where Are the Pollution Havens?", *Journal of Environment and Development*, Vol. 2(1).

Boyd, R., W. Hyde, and K. Kurita (1993): "Trade Policy and Environmental Accounting: A Case Study of Structural Adjustment and Deforestation in the Philippines", *mimeo*, Ohio University, Athens, Ohio.

de Bruyn, S., J. Van Den Bergh, and J. Opschoor. (1998): "Economic Growth and Emissions: Reconsidering the Empirical Basis of Environmental Kuznets Curves", *Ecological Economics*, Vol. 25(2), May.

Chakraborty, D. (2012): "Is India Turning into a Pollution Haven? Evidences from Trade and Investment Patterns", in Sacchidananda Mukherjee and Debashis Chakraborty (ed.): *Environmental Scenario in India: Successes and Predicaments*, Routledge, New York.

Chakrobarty, Pinaki. (2013): "Global Environmental Issues and Initiatives", in Rabindra N Bhattacharya (ed.): *Environmental Economics: An Indian Perspective*, Oxford University Press.

Chandrasekhar, C.P. (2011): "India's New, High-Growth Trajectory: Implications for Demand, Technology and Employment", *The Indian Journal of Labour Economics*, Vol. 54(1).

Chattopadhyay, S. (2005): "Dirtier Trade for India? Story of Globalization", *Contemporary Issues and Ideas in Social Sciences*, Vol. 1(3), November.

Cole, M.A., A.J. Rayner, and J.M. Bates. (1997): "The Environmental Kuznets Curve: An Empirical Analysis", *Environment and Development Economics*, Vol. 2.

Cole, M.A. (2003): "Development, Trade and the Environment: How Robust Is the Environmental Kuznets Curve?", *Environment and Development Economics*, Vol. 8(4).

Cole, M.A. (2006): "Does Trade Liberalization Increase National Energy Use?", *Economic Letters*, Vol. 92.

Cole, M.A., and A.J. Rayner. (2000): "The Uruguay Round and Air Pollution: Estimating the Composition, Scale and Technique Effects of Trade Liberalization", *Journal of International Trade and Economic Development*, Vol. 9(3).

Cole, M.A., and R.J.R. Elliott (2001): "Factor Endowments or Environmental Regulations? Determining the Trade-Environment Composition Effect", *Discussion Paper 01-06*, The University of Birmingham, Department of Economics.

Cole, M.A., J.R. Robert, and A.K. Azhar. (2001): "The Determinants of Trade in Pollution Intensive Industries: North-South Evidence", *Working Paper*, Department of Economics, University of Birmingham.

Cole, M.A., R.J.R. Elliot, and Jing Zhang (2008): "Growth, Foreign Direct Investment and the Environment: Evidence from Chinese Cities", weblink: *http://www.nottingham.ac.uk/cpi/documents/discussion-papers/discussion-paper-59-growth-fdi-environment.pdf*, accessed on 25-06-2014.

Consumer Unity and Trust Society (CUTS). (2003): "How Mining Companies Influence the Environment", *Briefing Paper No. 1*, Jaipur.

Copeland, B.R., and M.S. Taylor. (2003a): "Trade, Growth and the Environment", *NBER Working Paper 9823*, National Bureau of Economic Research, Cambridge, MA.

Copeland, B.R., and M.S. Taylor. (2003b): *Trade and the Environment: Theory and Evidence*, Princeton University Press, Princeton, NJ.

Cruz, W., and R. Repetto. (1993): *The Environmental Effects of Stabilization and Structural Adjustment Programs: The Philippines Case*, World Resources Institute, Washington, DC.

Daly, H. (1991): "Problems with Free Trade: Neoclassical and Steady State Perspectives", in D. Zaelke, P. Orbuch, and R. Housman (eds.): *Trade and Environment: Law, Economics and Policy*, Island Press, Washington, DC.

Das, Monica, and Sandwip K. Das. (2007): "Can Stricter Environmental Regulations Increase Export of the Polluting Good", *The B.E. Journal of Economic Analysis and Policy*, Vol. 7(1).

Dasgupta, S. A., S. Roy Mody, and D. Wheeler. (1995): "Environmental Regulation and Development: A Cross-Country Empirical Analysis", *World Bank*, Policy Research Department Working Paper No. 1448.

Dean, Judith M. (2002): "Does Trade Liberalization Harm the Environment? A New Test", *Canadian Journal of Economics*, Vol. 35(4).

Dean, Judith M., Mary E. Lovely, and Hua Wang. (2004): "Foreign Direct Investment and Pollution Havens: Evaluating the Evidence from China", Office of Economics Working Paper, U.S. International Trade Commission, *weblink:* http://ageconsearch.umn.edu/bitstream/15854/1/wp04001b.pdf, accessed 28-06-2014.

Deshpande, L.K., Alakh N Sharma, Anup K Karan, and Sandip Sarkar. (2004): *Liberalization and Labour: Labour Flexibility in Indian Manufacturing*, Institute for Human Development, New Delhi.

Dietzenbacher, E., and K. Mukhopadhyay. (2007): "An Empirical Examination of the Pollution Haven Hypothesis for India: Towards a Green Leontief Paradox?", *Environment and Resource Economics*, Vol. 36(4).

Dokadia, Afsha, and S. Pellissery. (2007): "Profits Without Loyalty: Is the Temporary Model Sustainable?", *The Indian Journal of Labour Economics*, Vol. 50(4).

Ederington, Josh, Arik Levinson, and Jenny Minier. (2004): "Trade Liberalization and Pollution Havens", Advances in Economic Analysis and Policy", *The B.E. Journals in Economic Analysis and Policy*, Vol. 4(2).

Eskeland, G. S., and A. E. Harrison. (1997): "Moving to Greener Pastures? Multinationals and the Pollution Haven Hypothesis", *Working Paper 1744*, Washington, DC: World Bank.

Eskeland, G.S., and A.E. Harrison. (2003): "Moving to Greener Pastures? Multinationals and the Pollution Haven Hypothesis?", *Journal of Development Economics*, Vol. 70(1).

Fieleke, N.S. (1975): "The Energy Content of US Export and Imports", *Working Papers No.51*, Div. Int. Finance, Board of Governors, Federal Reserve System.

Fredriksson, P.G. (1999): "The Political Economy of Trade Liberalization and Environmental Policy", *Southern Economic Journal*, Vol. (3), January.

Galeotti, M., and A. Lanza. (1999): "Richer and Cleaner? A Study on Carbon Dioxide Emissions in Developing Countries", *Proceedings from the 22nd IAEE Annual International Conference* (Rome), 9–12 June.

Gallagher, K. (2004): *Free Trade and the Environment: Mexico, NAFTA, and Beyond*, Stanford Law and Politics, Stanford University Press.

Gamper-Rabindran, S., and S. Jha. (2004): "Environmental Impact of India's Trade Liberalization", *Working Paper*, University of North Carolina at Chapel Hill, Department of Public Policy.

Georgescu-Roegen, N. (1971): *The Entropy Law and the Economic Process*, Harvard University Press, Cambridge.

Gerilla, G.P., S. Kagawa, and H. Inamura. (2002): "International Trade and Carbon Emissions: A Case of China and Japan", *Paper presented at the 14th International Conference on Input-Output Techniques held at UQAM*, Montreal, Canada, 10–15 October.

Greiner, A. (2005): "Fiscal Policy in an Endogenous Growth Model with Public Capital and Pollution", *Japanese Economic Review*, Vol. 56.

Grether, Jean-Marie, Nicole A. Mathys, and Jaime De Melo. (2007): "Is Trade Bad for the Environment? Decomposing World-wise SO2 Emissions 1990–2000", http://federation.ens.fr/ydepot/semin/texte0607/MEL2007TRA.pdf

Grossman, G., and A. Krueger. (1991): "Environmental Impacts of a North American Free Trade Agreement", *NBER Working Paper No. 3914*, Cambridge, MA.

Grossman, G. M., and A. B. Krueger. (1993): "Pollution and Growth: What Do We Know?", in I. Goldin and L. Winters (eds.): *The Economics of Sustainable Development*, MIT Press, Cambridge, MA.

Grossman, G. M., and A. B. Krueger. (1995): "Economic Growth and the Environment", *Quarterly Journal of Economics*, Vol. 110(2).

Gupta, Shreekant. (2000): "Impact of Trade and Investment Policies on the Environment with Reference to the Automobile Sector in India", *Mimeo.*

Gupta, Shreekant. (2002): "Environmental Benefits and Cost Savings Through Market-Based Instruments: An Application Using State-Level Data from India", *CDE Working Paper No. 111*, December.

Haan, M.D. (2002): "Extending the Scope of Environmental Indicators by Taking Into Account International Trade Dependencies", *Paper presented at the 14th International Conference on Input-Output Techniques held at UQAM*, Montreal, Canada, 10–15 October.

Hayami, H., and M. Nakamura. (2002): "CO_2 Emission of Alternative Technologies and Bilateral Trade between Japan and Canada: Relocating Production and an Implication for Joint Implementation", *Discussion Paper 75*, Keio Economic Observatory, Keio University, Japan.

Hettige, H, R.E.B. Lucas, and D. Wheeler. (1992): "The Toxic Intensity of Industrial Production: Global Patterns, Trends and Trade Policy", *American Economic Review*, Vol. 82(2).

Hirway, Indira, and Neha Shah. (2011): "Labour and Employment under Globalization: The Case of Gujarat", *Economic and Political Weekly*, Vol. XLVI(22), May 28, 2011.

Husted, B.W., and J.M. Logsdon. (1997): "The Impact of NAFTA on Mexico's Environmental Policy", *Growth and Change*, Vol. 28.

Jaffe, A., S. Peterson, P. Portney, and R. Stavins. (1993): *Environmental Regulations and the Competitiveness of US Industry*, Report Prepared for the US Department of Commerce, The Economic Resources Group, Cambridge, MA.

Jena, Pradyot R., N.C. Sahu, and Binayak Rath. (2005): "Does Trade Liberalization Create Pollution Haven? An Indian Experience", *Paper Presented at the International Conference on Environment and Development: Developing Countries Perspective*, 7–8 April, International Trade and Development Division, Jawaharlal Nehru University, New Delhi.

Jha, Shrehasi, and Shanti Gamper Rabindran. (2004): "Environmental Impact of India's Trade Liberalization", *https://www.gtap.agecon.purdue.edu/resources/download/1690.pdf*, accessed on 16-10-2014.

Jha, V. (1999): "Investment, Liberalization and Environmental Protection: Conflicts and Compatibilities in the Case of India", *Occasional Paper No. 1*, Cross Border Environmental Management Project, Copenhagen, Copenhagen Business School.

John, A., and R. Pecchennino. (1994): "An Overlapping Generations Model of Growth and the Environment", *The Economic Journal*, Vol. 104(427), November.

Kavossi, R. (1984): "Export Expansion and Economic Growth: Further Empirical Evidence", *Journal of Development Economics*, Vol. 14.

Kristrom, (2000): "On a Clear Day, You Might See the Environmental Kuznets Curve", Camp Resources (Wilmington, NC), 12–13 August 1999 and "Growth, Employment and the Environment", *Swedish Economic Policy Review*.

Kundu, A. (1997): "Trends and Structure of Employment in the 1990s: Implications for Urban Growth", *Economic and Political Weekly*, 14 June.

Lange, G.M., and R. Hasan. (2002): "Trade and the Environment in Southern Africa: The Impact of the 'User Pays' Principle for Water on Exports of Botswana, Namibia, and South Africa", *Paper Presented at the 14th International Conference on Input-Output Techniques held at UQAM*, Montreal, Canada, 10–15 October.

Lantz, V., and Q. Feng. (2006): "Assessing Income, Population and Technology Impacts on CO_2 emissions in Canada: Where's the EKC?", *Ecological Economics*, Vol. 57.

Lenzen, M. (2001): "A Generalized Input-Output Multiplier Calculus for Australia", *Economic Systems Research*, Vol. 13(1).

Levinson, Arik, and M. Scott Taylor. (2001): "Trade and Environment: Unmasking the Pollution Haven Effect", *Working Paper*, Georgetown University.

Lopez, R. (1994): "The Environment as a Factor of Production: The Effects of Economic Growth and Trade Liberalization", *Journal of Environmental Economics and Management*, Vol. 27(2), September.

Low, D., and A. Yates. (1992): "Do Dirty Industries Migrate", in P. Low (ed.): *International Trade and Environment*", World Bank, Washington.

Machado, G., R. Schaeffer, and E. Worrell. (2001): "Energy and Carbon Embodied in the International Trade of Brazil: An Input-Output Approach", *Ecological Economics*, Vol. 39(3).

Maler, K.G. (1993): "Economic Growth and the Environment", *Beijer International Institute of Ecological Economics Discussion Paper Series No.25.*

Mani, M., and David Wheeler. (1998): "In Search of Pollution Havens? Dirty Industry in the World Economy, 1960-1995", *Journal of Environment and Development*, Vol. 7(3), September.

Mani, M., and David Wheeler. (1999): "In Search of Pollution Havens? Dirty Industry in the World Economy", in Frederiksson (ed.): *Trade, Global Policy, and the Environment*, Washington, World Bank.

Mani, Muthukumara, and David Wheeler. (1997): "In Search of Pollution Havens? Dirty Industry in the World Economy, 1960–1999", *World Bank Working Paper No. 16*, April.

Mani, Muthukumara, and Shreyasi Jha. (2006): "Trade Liberalization and the Environment in Vietnam", *World Bank Policy Research Working Paper 3879*, April.

Mani, Muthukumara S. (1996): "Environmental Tariffs on Polluting Imports: An Empirical Study", *Environmental and Resource Economics*, Vol. 7.

Mathys, Nicole Andréa. (2004): "In Search of Evidence for the Pollution-Haven Hypothesis", Université de Neuchâtel, Division économique et sociale, June, weblink: *http://www.hec.unil.ch/nmathys/mem.pdf*, accessed on July 20, 2013.

McConnell, K. (1997): "Income and the Demand for Environmental Quality", *Environment and Development Economics*, Vol. 2, November.
Meadows, D.H., D.L. Meadows, J. Randers, and W.W. Behrens. (1972): *The Limits to Growth*, Earth Island Limited, London.
Merican, Yasmine, Zulkornain Yusop, Zaleha Mohd Noor, and Law Siong Hook. (2007): "Foreign Direct Investment and the Pollution in Five ASEAN Nations", *International Journal of Economics and Management*, Vol. 1(2).
Mukherjee, Sacchidanandaa, and Debashis Chakraborty. (2009): "Environment, Human Development and Economic Growth: A Contemporary Analysis of Indian States", *International Journal of Global Environmental Issues*, Vol. 9(1&2).
Mukhopadhyay, K. (2004): "Environmental Impacts of Trade with Europe: A Study on the Impact of Trade with EU on CO_2 Emissions in India during 1990s", *IDPAD Newsletter*, Vol. II(1), January–June.
Mukhopadhyay, K. (2006): "Impact on the Environment of Thailand's Trade with OECD Countries", *Asia-Pacific Trade and Investment Review*, Vol. 2(1), May.
Mukhopadhyay, K., and D. Chakraborty. (2004): "Environmental Impacts of Trade Liberalization in India", in D.M. Nachane, et al. (eds.): *Econometric Models: Theory and Applications*, Allied Publishers Limited.
Mukhopadhyay, K., and D. Chakraborty. (2005a): "Environmental Impacts of Trade in India", *International Trade Journal*, Vol. 19(2).
Mukhopadhyay, K., and D. Chakraborty. (2005b): "Is Free Trade Good for the Environment? Evidence from India", *Asia Pacific Development Journal*, Vol. 12(1).
Munasinghe, M. (1995): "Making Economic Growth More Sustainable", *Ecological Economics*, Vol. 15.
Munksgaard, J., and K.A. Pedersen. (2001): "CO_2 Accounts for Open Economies: Producer or Consumer Responsibility?", *Energy Policy*, Vol. 29(4).
Narayan, P.K., and S. Narayan. (2010): "Carbon dioxide Emissions and Economic Growth: Panel Data Emissions and Economic Growth: Panel Data Evidence from Developing Countries", *Energy Policy*, Vol. 38.
Olivier, J.G.J., and J.J.M. Berdowski. (2001): "Global Emissions Sources and Sinks", in J. Berdowski, R. Guicherit, and B.J. Heij (eds.): *The Climate System*, A.A. Balkema Publishers/Sweets and Zeitlinger Publishers, Lisse, The Netherlands.
Panayotou, T. (1997): "Demystifying the Environmental Kuznets Curve: Turning a Black Box into a Policy Tool", *Environment and Development Economics*, Vol. 2(4).
Panayotou, T. (2000): "Economic Growth and the Environment", *CID Working paper No. 60*, Harvard University.
Panayotou, T., and J.R. Vincent. (1997): "Environment and Competitiveness", *Global Development Report.*

Panayotou, T., and N. Islam. (1999): "Unveiling the Income-Environment Relationship: An Exploration into the Determinants of Environmental Quality", *Working Paper*, Department of Economics and Harvard Institute of International Development.

Papola, T.S. (2013): "Economic Growth and Employment Linkages: The Indian Experience", *ISID Working Paper no 2013/01*, New Delhi, January.

Pauli, F. (2003): "Environmental Kuznet Curve Investigation Using a Varying Coefficient AR-Model", *EEE Working Paper Series*, No. 2, December.

Perroni, C., and R.M. Wigle. (1994): "International Trade and Environmental Quality: How Important Are the Linkages?", *Canadian Journal of Economics*, Vol. 27.

Prakash, Aseem, and Matthew Potoski. (2006): "New Dependencies: FDI and the Cross-Country Diffusion of ISO 14001 Management Systems", weblink: *http://mba.tuck.dartmouth.edu/mechanisms/pages/Papers/prakash-potoski%20paper.pdf*, accessed on 01-02-2014.

Proops, J.L., G. Atkinson, B.F.V. Schlotheim, and S. Simon. (1999): "International Trade and the Sustainability Footprint: A Practical Criterion for Its Assessment", *Ecological Economics*, Vol. 28(1).

Przybylinski, M. (2002): "Bilateral 'Pollution Flows' between Poland and Germany", *Paper presented at the 14th International Conference on Input-Output Techniques held at UQAM*, Montreal, Canada, 10–15 October.

Ram, R. (1985): "Exports and Economic Growth: Some Additional Evidence", *Economic Development and Cultural Change*, Vol. 33.

Rock, M. (1996): "Pollution Intensity of GDP and Trade Policy: Can the World Bank Be Wrong?", *World Development*, Vol. 24(3).

Rock, M.T. (2002): *Pollution Control in East Asia: Lessons from Newly Industrializing Economies*, Resources for the Future Press, Washington D.C.

Sanyal, Kalyan. (2013): "International Trade and Environment", in Rabindra N Bhattacharya (ed.): *Environmental Economics: An Indian Perspective*, Oxford University Press.

Singh, Kavaljit. (1997): *The Reality of Foreign Investments: German Investment in India*, Madhyam Books, New Delhi.

Smarzynska, Beata, and S.J. Wei. (2004): "Pollution Haven and Foreign Direct Investment: Dirty Secret or Popular Myth? Contributions to Economic Analysis and Policy", *The B.E. Journals in Economic Analysis and Policy*, Vol. 3(2).

Stern, D.I. (2002): "Explaining Changes in Global Sulfur Emissions: An Econometric Decomposition Approach", *Ecological Economics*, Vol. 42.

Stern, D.I. (2004): "The Rise and Fall of the Environmental Kuznets Curve", *World Development*, Vol. 32.

Stern, D.I. (2005): "Global Sulfur Emissions Form 1850-2000", *Chemospere*, Vol. 58.

Stern, D.I. (2006): "Reversal of the Trend in Global Anthropogenic Sulfur Emissions", *Global Environmental Change*, Vol. 16.

Strutt, A., and K. Anderson. (1998): "Will Trade Liberalization Harm the Environment? The Case of Indonesia to 2020", *Seminar Paper 98-04*, Center for International Economic Studies, University of Adelaide.

Tewari, Meenu. (2000): "Trade Liberalization and the Restructuring of Tamil Nadu's Leather Sector: Coping with Liberalization's New Environmental Challenges and Lessons from Prior Episodes of Adjustment", *Working Paper*, CID, Harvard University.

Tobey, J.A. (1990): "The Effects of Domestic Environmental Policies on World Trade: An Empirical Test", *Kylos*, Vol. 43.

Unni, Jeemol, and Suma Scaria. (2009): "Governance Structure and Labour Market Outcomes in Garment Embellishment Chains", *The Indian Journal of Labour Economics*, Vol. 52(3).

Wadeskog, A. (2002): "Trade and the Environment in Input-Output Based Environmentally Accounts Analysis", *Paper presented at the 14th International Conference on Input-Output Techniques held at UQAM*, Montreal, Canada, 10–15 October.

Wagner, U., and C. Timmins. (2008): "Agglomeration Effects in Foreign Direct Investment and the Pollution Havens Hypothesis", *http://www.econ.duke.edu/~timmins/phavens.pdf*, accessed on 24-10-2013.

World Bank. (1992): *Development and the Environment*, World Development Report, Washington D.C.

Wright, D.J. (1974): "Goods and Services: An Input-Output Analysis", *Energy Policy*, Vol. 2(4).

Wyckoff, A.W., and J.M. Roop. (1994): "The Embodiment of Carbon in Imports of Manufactured Products: Implications for International Agreements on Greenhouse Gas Emissions", *Energy Policy*, Vol. 22(3).

Xing, Y., and C. Kolstad. (1997): "Do Lax Environmental Regulations Attract Foreign Investment?", *Environmental and Resource Economics*, Vol. 21.

CHAPTER 3

Methodology

Abstract The study adopts two approaches: (a) macro level and (b) micro level. The macro-level approach deals with examining the post-liberalization changes in the structure of manufacturing industries and estimation of industrial pollution loads for India as a whole. The micro-level approach deals with estimating the impact of pollution on social well-being at the village level. The chapter discusses the method of data collection, calculation of pollution loads and model specifications for estimating the impact of trade-led manufacturing growth on environment in terms of scale effect, composition effect and technique effect. An empirical model (ordinal logit model) is also constructed for estimating the impact of pollution on social well-being taking the case of Gujarat.

Keywords Macro level · Micro level · Model specification

The study adopts two approaches: (a) macro level and (b) micro level. The macro-level approach deals with examining the post-liberalization changes in the structure of manufacturing industries and estimation of industrial pollution loads for India as a whole. The micro-level approach deals with estimating the impact of pollution on the social well-being at the village level.

H. Jain, *Trade Liberalisation, Economic Growth and Environmental Externalities*, DOI 10.1007/978-981-10-2887-8_3

3.1 Macro-Level Approach

The macro-level approach is based upon the secondary sources of data. The data are collected in two phases: (i) for industry level and (ii) for environmental externalities. The trade liberalization has covered not only the trade of final goods but it is extended to investment flows, capital flows, technology flows and also development of intra-industry trade. On this basis, the trade liberalization is examined at the industry level as well as at the stages of processing. In order to know during which period the growth of FDI and technology transfer was high, the growth trend was compared for the 1990s and 2000s. Industry wise comparison was made to know the relationship of output, FDI and technology with international trade during the 1990s and 2000s. The flow of trade is determined on the basis of changes in India's relationship with its trading partners. The changes in the structures of industry over the period of post-reforms was determined in terms of trade openness, capital–labour ratio, FDI, share of high-tech industries in gross value added (GVA) and value added per worker. Further the inter-relationship between trade liberalization, trade orientation, FDI, capital–labour ratio and revealed comparative advantage is examined with the help of correlation coefficient.

3.1.1 Database

Two sets of data are prepared: one for the industrial level and other for the emission levels. The data for both the sets are collected from secondary sources for the years 1990–91, 1997–98, 2004–05 and 2009–10. The industry-level information for the output, fixed capital, employment and value added is obtained from the Annual Survey of Industries (ASI). The ASI data on output and fixed capital is in thousand rupees at current prices. In order to make the data comparable, the nominal values were deflated with the appropriate price indices after splicing. Industries were arranged as per the latest available National Industrial Classification (NIC 2008) and made comparable through concordance. Per capita income is obtained from Economic Survey.

The emission level for the industries is determined in terms of pollution loads. Since the developing countries lack sufficient data on pollution, the studies generally use the database from Industrial Pollution Projection System (IPPS) developed by World Bank in the early 1990s.[1] IPPS provides pollution intensities at the International Standard Industrial Classification

(ISIC) at 4- or 3-digit level. IPPS exploits the fact that industrial pollution is heavily affected by the scale of industrial activity, by its sectoral composition, and by the type of process technology used in production. It operates through sector estimates of pollution intensity (usually defined as pollution per unit of activity). IPPS combines data from industrial activities (such as output and employment) with data on pollution emissions to calculate the pollution intensity factors based on ISIC. IPPS covers about 1,500 product categories, all operating technologies, and hundreds of pollutants. It can project air, water, or solid waste emissions, and it incorporates a range of risk factors for human toxic and eco-toxic effects (Hettige et al. 1995).

3.1.2 Calculation of Pollution Load

Pollution loads for each industry are calculated from lower bound (LB) pollution intensities by medium with respect to total value of output. In the IPPS, pollution intensities (emission factors) are in pounds per US$ million at 1987 prices.

The following steps were used for calculating the pollution load:

I step: Mapping the NIC categories to ISIC codes.

II step: Converting IPPS pollution intensities to Indian Rupees (INR). In 1987–88, INR 12.966 = US$1 (Economic Survey, 2000–01). Also, 1 kg = 0.454 pounds. So dividing pollution intensity by 12.966 and multiplying by 0.454 gives us kilograms of pollutants per thousand INR in 1987–88.

III step: Inflating pollution intensity data to 2004–05 prices (base year). For this, the official wholesale price index (WPI) is used. The WPI is 44.26 (1990–91), 76.33 (1997–98), 100 (2004–05) and 126 (2009–10). Therefore, we used 2.26, 1.31, 1 and 0.79 as the inflation factor for the years 1990–91, 1997–98, 2004–05 and 2009–10, respectively, to obtain pollution intensities for selected years.

Pollution loads are calculated for air pollutants (SO_2, NO_2, CO, VOC, FP and TSP),[2] water pollutants (BOD and TSS)[3] and toxic pollutants (air, land and water). These loads were added to get the pollution load of each manufacturing industry.

According to Jha and Rabindran (2004), the pollution loads estimated using the IPPS database matches with that of Central Pollution

Control Board (CPCB) as there is a high degree of correlation (0.87) between the CPCB pollution intensity measures and IPPS pollution intensity measure for water pollution intensity and a moderate degree of correlation (0.46) between the air pollution intensity measures generated from the two sources. The CPCB do not have data on toxic pollution intensity.

3.1.3 *Model Specification for Estimating the Impact of Trade-Led Manufacturing Growth on Environment*

The environmental and trade economists have decomposed the total effect of trade on environment into scale, composition and technique effects (Grossman and Krueger, 1993; Gallagher, 2004 among others). Scale effect occurs when liberalization causes an expansion of economic activity (output). If the nature of that activity is unchanged but the scale is growing, then pollution and resource depletion will increase alongwith output. Composition effect occurs when increased trade leads nations to specialize in the sectors where they enjoy a comparative advantage. When comparative advantage is derived from differences in environmental stringency (i.e. the pollution haven effect), then the composition effect of trade will exacerbate existing environmental problems in the countries with relatively lax regulations. The opposite can be true when comparative advantage is a function of strong environmental controls. Technique effect, or changes in resource extraction and production technologies, can potentially lead to decline in pollution per unit of output for two reasons. First, the liberalization of trade and investment may encourage MNCs, who adhere to stricter environmental regulations in industrialized countries, can transfer cleaner technologies to developing countries. Second, if economic liberalization increases income levels, the newly affluent citizens may demand a cleaner environment (Gallagher 2004).

In the present study, the scale effect is measured by the scale of manufacturing activity per square kilometre of area for each industry. For measuring the composition effect, capital–labour ratio[4] is used as a proxy variable. Technique effect is captured by GNP per capita.[5] Since the pollution policy responds slowly, if at all, to changes in income levels, we use one period lagged, 3 years moving average of income per capita. The scale effect on pollution is reflected from the manufacturing activity taking place within the country while the technique effect should reflect from the income of residents irrespective of where it is earned.

The pollution concentration also depends upon the local factors like population, education and skill, awareness about pollution, infrastructure, world relative price of dirty goods and abatement technology. These factors change slowly with time. Some of them are observable and some are unobservable. Choosing these variables or their proxies will generate new issues of data quality, coverage, etc. Considering that these variables affect the emission of pollutants, we have captured them through an unrestricted time dummy.

The regression results are obtained by using a pooled cross-section method on a list of industries for the selected years.

To explain the variations in pollution loads, three models are constructed as follows:

Model	*Nature of model*	*Equations*
Model A	Linear	$PL = \alpha + \beta_1 MNA + \beta_2 KLR + \beta_3 PCI + TD$
Model B	Non-linear	$PL = \alpha + \beta_1 MNA + \beta_2 KLR + \beta_3 (KLR)^2 + \beta_4 PCI + \beta_5 (PCI)^2 + \beta_6 PCI \times KLR + TD$
Model C	Non-linear	$PL = \alpha + \beta_1 MNA + \beta_2 (MNA)^2 + \beta_3 KLR + \beta_4 (KLR)^2 + \beta_5 PCI + \beta_6 (PCI)^2 + \beta_7 PCI \times KLR + TD$

Here PL = industrial pollution load (calculated from IPPS coefficients),
MNA = manufacturing activity (= GDP/km^2 area),
KLR = capital–labour ratio (Real fixed capital/no. of persons engaged),
PCI = real per capita income,
TD = time dummy.

The above models are regressed for SO_2 and NO_2 as both these pollutants account for the highest share in total pollution load of manufacturing industries.

Model A assumes linearity in response to scale, technique and composition variables. Theoretically, the impact of capital accumulation on pollution depends on the techniques of production in place. Since trade liberalization alters the factor composition as well as income, the impact of capital accumulation on the composition of output cannot be considered as a linear function of capital–labour ratio. Similarly, the impact of income gains on pollution depends on the existing composition of output and hence the existing capital–labour ratio and income per capita. To account for these possibilities, model A is amended by adding the square of the per capita income and capital–labour ratio (model B). Also the combined effect of capital–labour ratio and per capita income is captured by their cross product. Further non-linearity is considered by adding square of MNA to model B (model C). A non-linearity in the impact of scale could arise from non-homotheticicities in production or consumption (Antweiler et al. 2001)

3.2 Micro-Level Approach

Micro-level approach is based on primary data collected with the help of household-based[6] survey during the year 2013 (June–July). The study area consists of the villages surrounding the two industries, namely petroleum refinery in Jamnagar (Region 1) and fertilizer and chemical industry in Vadodara (Region 2) of Gujarat (Fig. 3.1). The selection of these industries is on the basis of their industrial output and pollution loads after the economic reforms. In Gujarat, after ranking the industries for their pollution loads, these industries stand at second and fourth position respectively. The sample size consists of 100 households (50 from Region 1 and 50 from Region 2) surrounding the selected industries in a radius of 10 km. The sample was selected through purposive random sampling technique. The study is focused only on the farmers who are practising agriculture since last 20 years or more as they can better respond to the changing agricultural productivity after the establishment of industries. Since the study is focused on the agricultural impact of industrial emissions due to selected industries, those households were dropped who are living in the selected villages but have their agricultural land in some other village that is not in the 10 km vicinity of the selected industry. The reason is that the impact of emission decreases with increase in distance. Even those villages, which are in a radius of 10 km, but close to some other industry from the other side, could not become the part of this study. These villages could have combined effects of emissions from more than one industry. The location of the selected villages is shown in Fig. 3.1. The detail about the sample selected is given in Annexure (A 3.2).

The information at the household level was collected with the help of structured questionnaire (Annexure A 3.1). Discussion was also held with the other households and officials at panchayat level to probe into the issue. Most of the information obtained from the farmers was based upon approximations especially for 10 years before. The validity of information

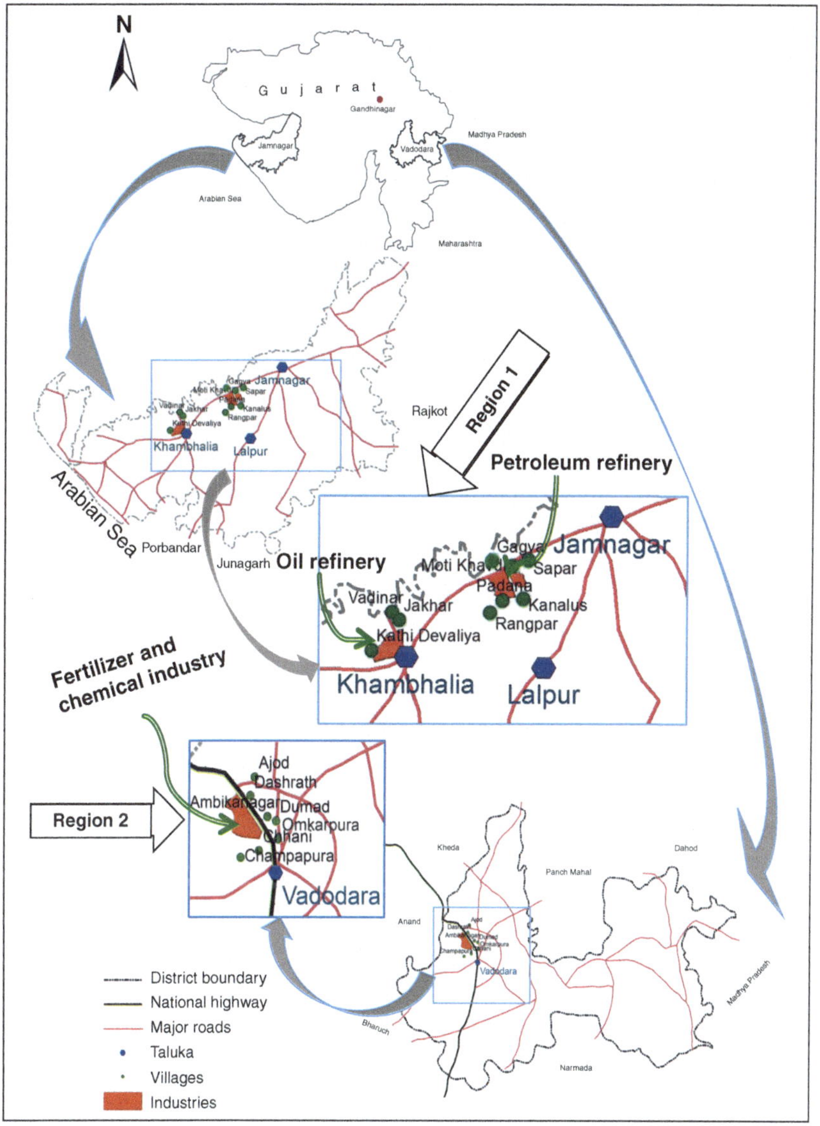

Fig. 3.1 Location of study villages surrounding the selected industries

was cross-checked. Besides educational status of the household,[7] housing status, awareness generating assets owned by the household and agricultural assets owned by the household were indexed on the basis of their available numbers. Instead of calculating the monetary value of the assets, it was thought of counting them. For the rural farmers, having an asset is more important than its monetary value. Some of the information especially on industrial pollution was response based and qualitative in nature. Therefore, in order to maintain the symmetry, all the variables were given ordinal numbers (as shown in Table 3.1).

3.2.1 *Empirical Model*

The decrease in agricultural productivity is examined by estimating the ordinal logit model,[8,9] (OLM) which is based upon the assumption that the disturbance term u_i follows the logistic distribution (Gujarati 2011). This model better suits to handle the ordinal scale variables.

The model is of the following form:

$$Y^* = \sum B_k X_{ik} + U_i \tag{3.1}$$

where Y^* is unobserved (extent of decrease in agricultural productivity), the *X*s are the regressors and u_i is the error term.

In this study, there are 50 independent individuals (or observations) for each industry and they face *J* ordered ($J = 3$) categories (low, moderate and high).[10] These categories are separated by the threshold parameter[11] or cut-off, the *a*s.

$$\begin{aligned} Y_i &= 1, \text{if } Y_i^* \leq a_1 \\ Y_i &= 2, \text{if } a_1 \leq Y_i^* \leq a_2 \\ Y_i &= 3, \text{if } Y_i^* \geq a_2 \end{aligned} \tag{3.2}$$

The method of estimation in OLM is based upon the principle of maximum likelihood.

$$Pr(Y_i \leq j) = Pr\left(B_1 X_{1i} + B_2 X_{2i} + \ldots + B_k X_{ki} + u_i \leq a_j\right) \tag{3.3}$$

$$= Pr\left(u_i \leq a_j - B_1 X_{1i} - B_2 X_{2i} - \ldots - B_k X_{ki}\right) \tag{3.4}$$

Table 3.1 Description of the independent variables

Variable	*Description*	*Hypothesized sign*
Demographic characteristics		
Caste	=1 if SC	+
	=2 if OBC	–
	=3 if General	–
Age of head farmer	=1 if between 27 and 46 years	+/–
	=2 if between 46 and 65 years	–
	=3 if > 65 years	+/–
Occupational structure of the household		
Percentage of family members engaged in non-agriculture activity	=1 if < 27 %	+
	=2 if 27 to 54 %	+
	=3 if > 54 %	+
Percentage of females plus senior citizens engaged in agriculture	=1 if < 20 %	+/–
	=2 if 20 to 40 %	+
	=3 if > 40 %	+
Status of the household		
Educational status	=1 if low	+
	=2 if moderate	+/–
	=3 if high	+/–
Housing status	=1 if low	+
	=2 if moderate	+/–
	=3 if high	+/–
Awareness generating assets owned by the household	=1 if less	–
	=2 if moderate	–
	=3 if more	–
Agricultural status of the household		
Land size	=1 if ≤ 2.5 acre	+
	=2 if 2.5 to 5 acre	+/–
	=3 if > 5 acre	–
Agricultural assets owned	=1 if less	–
	=2 if moderate	–
	=3 if more	–
Pollution-related variables		
Source of irrigation	=1 if irrigation by well	+
	=0 otherwise[13]	+/–
Industrial pollution	=1 if low	+
	=2 if moderate	+
	=3 if high	+
Distance of village from the industry	=1 if ≤ 2.5 km	+
	=2 if 2.5 to 5 km	+
	=3 if 5 to 7.5 km	+/–

Equation (3.4) gives the (cumulative probability) that Y_i falls in a category j and below (i.e. in category 1, 2 or 3). The cumulative distribution function (CDF) of the logistic probability distribution is given by

$$\frac{exp(a_j - BX)}{1 + exp(a_j - BX)} \tag{3.5}$$

BX stands for $\Sigma B_k X_k$.

The effect of a regressor on the ordered dependent variable is non-linear, as it gets channelled through a non-linear CDF.[12] Since the outcomes in Equation (3.2) reflect the ordering of the response scales the odds ratio are defined as

$$\frac{Pr[Y_j \leq j|x]}{Pr[Y_j > j|x]} = \frac{Pr[Y_j \leq j|x]}{Pr[1 - Pr(Y_i \leq j|x)]} \tag{3.6}$$

where

$$\Pr[Y_i \leq j|X] = \sum_{m=1}^{j} Pr[Y_i = m|X] \tag{3.7}$$

which denotes the cumulative probability that the outcome is less than or equal to j.

Using Equation (3.5) to compute the odds ratio in Equation (3.6) and taking the log, we obtain

$$\begin{aligned} \text{logit}[\Pr(\text{Yi} \leq \text{j})] &= \ln\frac{\Pr(\text{Yi} \leq \text{j})}{\Pr(\text{Yi} > \text{j})} = \ln\frac{\Pr(\text{Yi} \leq \text{j})}{[1 - \Pr(\text{Yi} \leq \text{j})]} \\ &= a_j - \sum b_k X_{ik},\ j = 1, 2, 3 \end{aligned} \tag{3.8}$$

The logit in Equation (3.8) is linear in a as well as B.

For comparison of the empirical results, the marginal effects or partial derivatives are computed as

$$\frac{\partial P}{\partial X_{ik}} = B_j$$

The partial derivative indicates the impact of regressor on the probability of decrease in agricultural productivity. That is holding all other variables constant, for a unit increase in X_k, the probability of Y_i^* is expected to change by B_j units.

3.2.1.1 Variables

Dependent variable

The decrease in agricultural productivity is explained by indexing the crop-wise decrease in productivity during the last 10 years. The obtained index was further classified into three categories: low, moderate and high indicating the different levels of decrease in productivity.

Independent variables

The decrease in agricultural productivity in a region is determined by various regional and household-specific factors like demographic characteristics, household status, occupational structure of the household, status of the household, agricultural characteristics and industrial pollution. The variables selected to explain the variations in agricultural productivity are as follows:

1. **Caste** is a demographic variable but it reflects the social status of the household in the village. A person having a high social status is entitled to more social rights and benefits. This should have a positive effect on the economic activity of the household. Besides the caste based occupational division is still persisting in the villages. Agricultural activity is basically ascribed to the general and OBC classes. Therefore, practising agriculture can be considered to be the inherited skill for these classes. Hence, other things remaining the same, more the number of general and OBC (other backward caste) farmers, lesser should be the decrease in productivity. People belonging to lower social status generally have low skill with less or no accessibility to physical resources. Their higher involvement in agriculture should indicate poor agricultural productivity.
2. **Age of the head farmer** is an indicator of the level of experience in agricultural activity. A more experienced person knows all the ifs and buts of the agricultural performance and can take steps to mitigate the risks. Therefore, other things remaining the same,

higher the age of the head farmer, lesser should be the decrease in agricultural productivity. But for senior citizens, the contribution and experience values if the age is associated with good mental and physical health. Regarding the young age group, the learning is associated with education, mobility, exposure, social interaction, etc. which enhances the productivity.

3. **Involvement of family members in non-agricultural activities** mainly comprises the adult males in the family. Ceteris paribus, their hard work in agriculture could result into an increased productivity. But this group has the tendency to seek for more remunerative jobs. Their more involvement in non-agricultural activity should imply more decrease in agricultural productivity.
4. **Involvement of females and senior citizens in agriculture** increases only if the income from agriculture is scarce to run the household activity. The young and adult male members go out for work, leaving the agricultural land for the females and senior citizens in the family. In this situation, agriculture is treated as a residual activity. Therefore, greater involvement of females and senior citizens in agriculture should indicate that there is a higher decrease in agricultural productivity.
5. **Educational status** of the family depends upon the number of members having primary, secondary or college-level education. The more the family members with higher education, the higher is the educational status of the family. The higher the educational status, the higher is the level of awareness. Keeping the other variables constant, a higher level of educational status leads to new ideas that can be applied to raise the agricultural productivity. But if the agricultural productivity becomes non-viable, there is high possibility of this group to move to some other remunerative jobs. Therefore, the agricultural productivity is mainly associated with less educated persons. Due to their poor skill, they have less chances of leaving the agriculture. Therefore, the lower the educational status of the household, the higher is the decrease in agricultural productivity.
6. **Housing status** is determined from the decent housing space including rooms, kitchen, verandah, store room, bathroom, toilet, outer space, terrace and washing space. A decent housing space indicates the better status of the household. This reflects the accessibility of the household to better seeds and fertilizer. Keeping the

other things constant, better the housing status, lesser is the decrease in agricultural productivity and vice versa. A better housing status means a better quality of life. This implies less involvement of the family members in agricultural farm. Rather, they give the farm on contract or in the hands of labourers and get engaged in other non-farm activity. The more they loose their hold in agriculture, the greater is the decrease in agricultural productivity.

7. **Awareness generating assets** owned by the household include television, dish connection, mobile/landline phone, computer, internet, two wheeler and four wheeler. Various types of programmes meant for farmers are telecasted on TV. This increases farmers' awareness about the new methods of agriculture. These assets through social networking, makes the person aware of the upcoming risks and uncertainties. Other things remaining the same, a high level of exposure decreases the risk in agricultural productivity.
8. **Size of agricultural land** decreases when it is diverted to non-agricultural uses. This hinders with the optimal utilization of agricultural inputs. As a result, the marginal productivity of the farm decreases and thus the agricultural practice becomes a non-viable operation. Thus the decrease in the land size should indicate higher decrease in agricultural productivity.
9. **Agricultural assets** smoothens practising agriculture and makes it cost-effective. Other things remaining the same, the lesser the agricultural assets owned by the household, the lesser should be the agricultural productivity.
10. **Major source of irrigation** is the underground water in all the selected villages. Due to subsidized electricity for agriculture, underground water is extracted through borewells. But if the underground water depletes due to industrial emission or any other source, it will affect the agricultural productivity. The large farmers generally irrigate their land by wells. But it is not cost-effective for the small farmers. Therefore, the major part of the small and marginal farms depends upon rain water or surface water like river and canals. These sources are comparatively less polluted. Therefore, it can be said that the greater the irrigation by wells, the greater is the possibility of decrease in productivity.
11. **Industrial pollution** generally takes place by discharge of untreated waste water into the ground or discharging it through water streams. It may also occur by releasing of smoke into the air

that gets deposited on the crop and trees. The result is decrease in the fertility of land. Besides the release of smoke into the air burns the crop leaves as well as standing crops. Even the flowers do not stay for long. For some crops, the flowering process decreases. Therefore, higher pollution intensity should mean higher decrease in agricultural productivity.

12. **Distance of village from the industry** also determines the severity of impact of pollution on well-being. The impact of pollution decreases with distance. Therefore, those villages near to the industry are more prone to have the effect of pollution and more decrease in agricultural productivity.

Notes

1. See Hettige et al. (1995).
2. Sulphur dioxide (SO_2), nitrogen dioxide (NO_2), carbon monoxide CO), volatile organic compounds (VOC), fine particulates (FP) and total suspended particulates (TSP).
3. Biological oxygen demand (BOD), total suspended solids (TSS).
4. Capital–labour ratio measured as fixed capital per worker, reflects the mechanization of the production process of a particular industry during a fiscal year.
5. See Antweiler (2001) for detail.
6. Household is the basic decision-making unit for the allocation of family labour between various economic and non-economic activities. The household takes this decision on the basis of cost and benefits of an economic activity. If the activity is remunerative, majority of the family labour will be engaged in that activity, otherwise they try to shift to some other remunerative activity.
7. Educational status of the household was determined by giving appropriate weights to the household member according to the level of education (up to 5th standard, 5th to 10th standard and above 10th standard) and then indexed.
8. Polytomous universal model method (PLUM), Statistical Package for the Social Sciences.
9. Also known as Proportional Odd Model.
10. We observe an individual Y_i in one of the three-ordered categories. The OLM estimates not only the coefficients of the X regressors but also the threshold parameter.

11. These threshold parameters demarcate the boundaries of the various categories. The slope coefficients of the *X* regressors are the same in each category; it is only that their intercepts (cut-offs) differ. In other words, we have parallel regression lines (surfaces), but they are anchored on different intercepts. That is why OLM are also known as proportional odd models (Gujarati 2011).
12. CDFs are elongated S-shaped curves, which are obviously non-linear.
13. Other sources of irrigation are river and pond. If the toxic waste is discharged into river and pond, the agricultural productivity will decrease.

References

Annual Survey of Industries, weblink: http://mospi.nic.in/

Antweiler, W., B.R. Copeland, and M.S. Taylor. (2001): "Is Free Trade Good for the Environment?", *American Economic Review*, Vol. 91(4).

Economic Survey. GOI, weblink: http://indiabudget.nic.in

Gallagher, K. (2004): *Free Trade and the Environment: Mexico, NAFTA, and Beyond*, Palo Alto, Stanford Law and Politics, Stanford University Press.

Grossman, G.M., and A.N. Krueger. (1993): "Environmental Impact of a North American Free Trade Agreement", *NBER Working Paper No. 3914*, Cambridge MA.

Gujarati, D. (2011): *Econometrics by Example*, Palo Alto, Palgrave Macmillan.

Hettige, H., P. Martin, M. Singh, and D. Wheeler. (1995): "The Industrial Pollution Projection System (IPPS) Policy Research", *Working Paper No. 1431* (part 1 and 2), The World Bank, Policy Research Department, Environment, Infrastructure and Agriculture Division, March.

Jha, Shrehasi, and Shanti Gamper Rabindran. (2004): "Environmental Impact of India's Trade Liberalization", *https://www.gtap.agecon.purdue.edu/resources/download/1690.pdf*, accessed on 16-10-2014.

CHAPTER 4

Trade Liberalization Process and India's Growth Experiences

Abstract Trade liberalization enables the country to compete with other countries. The increase in competition directs the resources from less advantageous activity to more advantageous activity. The efficient allocation of resources enhances productivity. Considering the importance of trade in the growth process, India's post-liberalization growth experiences are highly influenced by its restructured trade pattern. This chapter captures these experiences by focusing on trade liberalization process and emerging pattern of India's external trade. The chapters includes an overview of India's trade liberalization process, tariff policy according to industrial products and stages of processing; trends and patterns of FDI flow in Indian industries; foreign technology transfers; post-liberalized experiences in terms of exports, imports and trading partners; and relationship between India's post-reforms growth and instruments of trade liberalization using elasticity coefficients.

Keywords Trade liberalization process · Tariff policy · FDI · Foreign technology transfers · India's international trade experiences

The economic reforms, which began on a bold and firm footing during the year 1991, aimed to replace a centrally controlled, protectionist economic regime with a competitive environment. As per neo-liberal thinking, more openness and free interaction of market forces in trade-related activities

H. Jain, *Trade Liberalisation, Economic Growth and Environmental Externalities*, DOI 10.1007/978-981-10-2887-8_4

imparts both efficiency and dynamism to the industrial growth process. On this basis, an outward-looking policy (particularly in the sphere of trade) extended the process of liberalization towards flows of investment, technology and finances.

Considering the importance of trade in the growth process, India's post-liberalization growth experiences are highly influenced by its restructured trade pattern. The present chapter captures these experiences by focusing on trade liberalization process and the emerging pattern of India's external trade. The chapter is structured as follows: Section 4.1 gives an overview of the trade liberalization process in India. Section 4.2 examines India's tariff policy according to industrial products and stages of processing. Section 4.3 discusses the trends and patterns of FDI flow in Indian industries. Section 4.4 focuses on foreign technology transfers. Section 4.5 deals with India's post-liberalized trade experiences in terms of export, import and trading partners. Section 4.6 relates India's post-reforms growth with trade liberalization. Section 4.7 concludes the chapter.

4.1 Trade Liberalization Process in India

India's post-independence development strategy was one of national self-sufficiency and stressed the importance of government regulation of the economy. In particular, with high nominal tariffs and extensive non-tariff barriers, India's trade regime was one of the most restrictive in Asia. The regime included a complex structure of import licensing, an actual user policy through which imports were restricted by intermediaries, restrictions of certain exports and imports to the public sector (canalization), phased manufacturing programmes that mandated progressive import substitution and government purchase preferences for domestic producers (Topavala and Khandelwal 2010). The only exceptions were commodities listed in the Open General License (OGL) category capital goods were divided into a restricted category and the OGL category. While import licences were required for restricted capital goods, those in the OGL could be imported without a licence subject to several conditions. The most important of these were that the importing firm had to be the 'actual user' of the equipment and could not sell the latter for 5 years without the permission of the licensing authorities and that the resulting change in capacity must be compatible with the capacity approved by industrial licensing authorities. Intermediate goods were divided into banned, restricted and limited permissible categories plus an OGL category. As the names suggest, the first three lists were in order of import licensing stringency; OGL imports of intermediate goods were also governed by the 'actual user' condition. The import of consumer goods were, however, banned (except those which were considered 'essential' and could only be imported by the designated government canalizing agencies) (Chand and Sen 2002).

During the 1980s, India embarked on market reforms to ease import and industrial licences. However, during this period, trade policy remained restrictive. By the end of the 1980s, only 12 per cent of manufactured products could be imported under an open general licence and the average tariff was still among the highest in Asia at more than 90 per cent (Cerra and Saxena 2000).[1] Furthermore, the average effective tariff rate for capital goods increased from 37 per cent in 1973–74 to 63 per cent in 1988–89. Also consumer goods remained in the banned list for the entire duration of the 1970s and 1980s. The pace of trade reforms, in particular, the shift from quantitative import controls to a protective system based on tariffs – initiated in the mid-1970s were considerably quickened by the new government (led by Rajiv Gandhi) that came into power in November 1984. Also, beginning in the mid-1980s, there was a renewed emphasis by the new administration on export promotion. The number and value of incentives offered to the exporters were increased and their administration streamlined. The allotment of REP licences – tradable import entitlements awarded to exporters on a product-specific basis – became increasingly generous (Agarwal and Goldar 1995). At the same time, the exchange rate became an important tool of export promotion and there was a steady devaluation of the Indian rupee during this period. The latter may have counteracted the decrease in protection brought about the liberalization of import controls in the Indian manufacturing sector (Chand and Sen 2002).

However, concurrent to the gradual liberalization of the late 1980s was a rise in macroeconomic imbalances – namely, fiscal and balance of payment deficits – which increased India's vulnerability to shocks. As a result, the sudden increase in oil prices due to the Gulf War in 1990, the drop in remittances from Indian workers in the Middle East, slackened demand of important trading partners, and political uncertainty, all served to undermine investor confidence and resulted in large capital outflows. To deal with its external payments problems in 1991, India turned to the International Monetary Fund (IMF) for assistance. Financial assistance from the IMF was conditional. The IMF support was on macroeconomic stabilization[2] policies and structural adjustment reforms,[3] of which liberalizing trade was a key component.[4] As a result, over a short period of time, India drastically reduced tariffs and narrowed the dispersions in tariff across sectors and also renewed quantitative restrictions (QRs) on imported inputs and capital goods for export production (Chopra et al. 1995). The government's trade policy under the Eighth Five-Year Plan (1992–97) ushered in radical changes to the trade regime by sharply reducing the role of the import and export control system. The share of products subject to QRs decreased from 87 per cent in 1987–88 to 45 per cent in 1994–95, and actual user condition on imports was discontinued. Furthermore, all 26 import licensing were eliminated and a negative list was established (Hasan et al. 2003). Thus, apart from goods in the negative list, all goods could be imported without licences (Goldar 2002).

In addition to easing import and export restrictions, tariffs were drastically reduced. The average tariffs fell from more than 87 percentage points in 1990 to 43 percentage points in 1996, and the standard deviation of tariffs dropped by about 30 per cent during the same period. The reform changed the structure of protection across industries (Topavala and Khandelwal 2010). There were also changes in the exchange rates. The Indian rupee was devalued 20 per cent against the US dollar in July 1991 and further devalued in February 1992 when an explicit dual exchange market was introduced. Despite the devaluation, which by itself would have been expected to have an import reducing effect, imports were expected to grow substantially and create competitive pressures within the Indian market, due to even larger reduction in tariffs and quantitative restrictions (Krishna and Mitra 1998).

India remained committed to further trade liberalization, and since 1997, there have been further adjustments to import tariffs. However, at the time the government announced the export–import policy in the Ninth Plan (1997–2002), the sweeping reforms outlined in the previous plan had been undertaken and pressures for further reforms from external sources had abated. In most cases, these measures went all beyond the country's commitments in this regard to the WTO. Thus, despite tariff bindings of as much as 150 per cent in particular sectors, and average tariff bindings of around 80 to 100 per cent, the average rate of tariffs in the Indian economy in 2004 was only around 20 per cent (Ghosh 2006). The chief purpose of this was to bring domestic relative prices into line with world prices, thereby supposedly creating conditions for greater efficiency and competitiveness of domestic production.

This in turn was supposed to generate more rapid increase in exports, which was expected to shift towards more labour-intensive forms of production (Ghosh 2006).

4.2 Tariff Policy in India Since 1991

The dismantling of protection started with tariff reduction. Figure 4.1 shows that average tariff protection for all products declined from a high rate of 81 per cent in 1990 to a low rate of 12 per cent by 2010–11. The decrease in tariff rates is greater for industrial products as compared to agricultural products. As revealed from the graph, the industrial sector face an average tariff rate of less than 10 per cent while it is 33.2 per cent for agricultural sector. Peak tariffs for industrial products were cut down from over 200 per cent in 1990 to 30 per cent in 2001 and finally to 1 per cent in 2012 (Annexure A4.1). This indicates that industrial sector received considerable importance in tariff reduction efforts under the ambit of trade liberalization policy.

Among the industrial products, as shown in Table 4.1, tariff rates have significantly decreased for all the products since 1990. Currently, mineral products are facing a tariff rate of less than 5 per cent and machines and electricals, petroleum, chemical and metal products face a tariff rate in the range of 6 to 8 per cent. For textiles and clothing, wood and miscellaneous products, the tariff rate is 9 to 10 per cent. Food products, animal products and transportation appears to be a somewhat protected

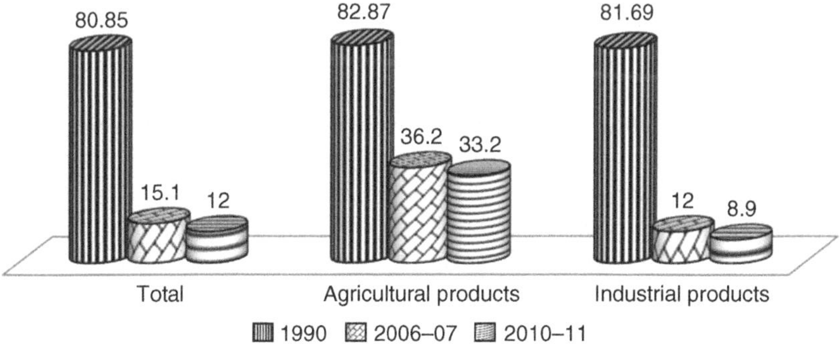

Fig. 4.1 Average tariff rates by sectors (MFN applied) *Source*: WITS database; WTO Secretariat Solution

Table 4.1 Tariff rates according to industrial products (MFN applied)

Industrial product	*1990*	*1997*	*2005*	*2010/11*
Animal	67.94	14.43	31.09	29.5
Chemicals	76.24	29.2	15.58	8.1
Food products	117.21	50.65	42.53	40.48
Footwear	100	40	15	10
Petroleum	46	19.45	14.42	8.2
Machine and electricals	79.1	25.16	13.56	6.9
Metals	91.79	28.53	16.46	7.32
Minerals	60.32	20.51	11.7	4.92
Miscellaneous	87.8	31.43	14.17	9.03
Plastic or rubber	95.24	33.05	15.34	9.64
Stone and glass	86.32	38.69	15	9.84
Textiles and clothing	95.15	38.15	24.95	10
Transportation	60.27	33.02	23.87	21.5
Wood, pulp, paper and furniture	77.12	24.06	13.41	9.07

Source: WITS database, WTO Secretarial Calculations

sector as they have tariff rates above 20 per cent. The picture reflects that the tariff rates declined sharply for importing those products which are important for boosting the manufacturing activities. These are minerals, machines and electricals, chemicals, petroleum, metals and wood.

Even within the manufacturing industry, the tariff rate varied according to the nature of manufacturing good. Figure 4.2 shows that during the early years of the 1990s, the tariff rates for all types of goods declined but it was kept comparatively low for raw materials. Since 2000 onwards, the focus shifted to increase the import of capital goods followed by intermediate goods. The tariff rate for capital goods decline from 51 per cent in 1992 to 8.3 per cent by 2009 and that of intermediates declined from 60 per cent in 1992 to 13 per cent in 2009. Raw material is still facing a tariff rate of 21 per cent. Although nominal tariff on consumer goods was reduced in line with those on other goods, the effective rate of tariffs on consumer goods actually have increased for much of the 1990s because the remaining import restrictions kept the effective rate of tariff protection high on final consumer goods (Veermani 2012). Consequently, the consumer goods sector was kept somewhat insulated from competition. During the 1990s when the definition of consumer goods was changed to suit the importer's needs, tariffs were relaxed for the import of parts, components and

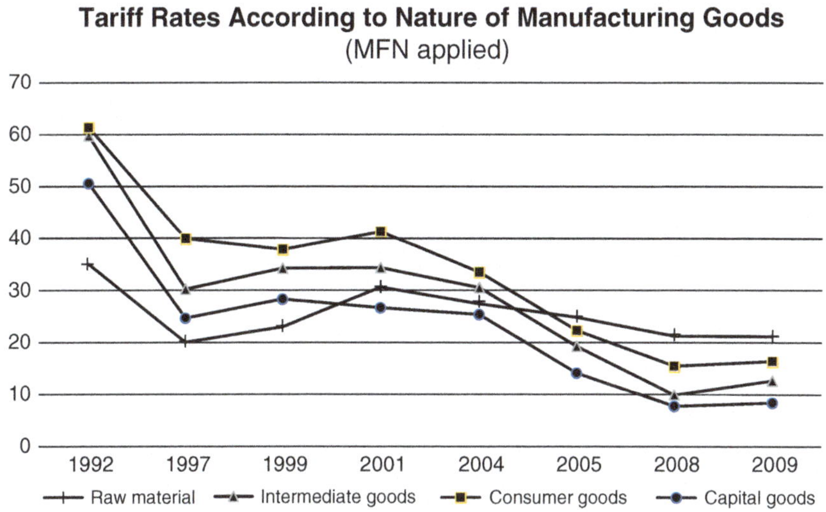

Fig. 4.2 Tariff rates according to nature of manufacturing goods (MFN applied)
Source: WITS Database

spares of consumer goods as well. Further, the list of free importable was expanded and by 1995, more than 3,000 tariff lines covering raw material, intermediates and capital goods were freed from import licensing requirements. Further, studies estimating the ERP and import coverage ratio showed that as compared with the 1980s, ERP declined in the 1990s. It declined from 125.9 per cent in 1986–90 to 82.2 per cent in 1990–95 and further to 40.4 per cent in 1996–2000, while import coverage ratio declined from 96.1 per cent in 1986–90 to 37.9 per cent in 1990–95 and further to 24.8 per cent in 1996–2000 (Das 2003). More important, however, was that QRs were removed for all items in 2001. Also some important export incentives were announced, such as the enhancement of import replenishment (REP) licence entitlements to 30 per cent across-the-board for all merchandise exporters, which are later raised to 40 per cent for some sectors.

Table 4.2 shows the average effective tariff rates by stages of processing. The average tariff rates for all the stages of manufacturing have decreased. The tariff rates has decreased faster for the semi-processed goods (from 122 % in 1990–91 to 8.6 % in 2010–11) followed by

Table 4.2 Average tariffs by stages of processing, 1990–91 to 2010–11 (in %)

Years	*Unprocessed*	*Semi-processed*	*Fully processed*
1990–91	107	122	130
1993–94	50	75	73
1995–96	27	44	43
1996–97	25	38	42
1997–98	25	35	37
2006–07	23.6	11.7	15.8
2010–11	22.5	8.6	12.2
% change (1990/91–2010/11)	83.66	92.95	90.61

Source: (1) TPRI, 2010–11
(2) WTO Secretariat Calculations, based on data provided by the Indian authorities

processed goods (from 130 % in 1990–91 to 12.2 % in 2010–11) and unprocessed goods (from 107 % in 1990–91 to 22.5 % in 2010–11).

As a whole, decreasing the tariff barriers on intermediate and semi-processed goods reflects an impetus for developing intra-industry trade linkages and that on capital goods reflects making the Indian manufacturing industries more capital intensive.

4.3 Foreign Direct Investment in India: Trends and Patterns

FDI is generally known to be the most stable component of capital flows needed to finance current account deficit. At the macro level, FDI is a non-debt-creating source of additional external finances and their returns depends on the performance of projects financed by investors. In fact, FDI provides a win-win situation to both the host and the home countries. The home countries want to take advantage of the vast markets opened by industrial growth. On the other hand, the host countries aim at acquiring technological and managerial skills and supplement domestic savings and foreign exchange. Moreover, in order to overcome the deficiencies of all kinds of resources viz., financial, capital, entrepreneurship, technological know-how, skills and practices, access to markets abroad for their economic development, developing nations accepted FDI as a sole visible panacea for all their scarcities (Bhattacharya 2012).

In India, the progressive liberalization process over two decades coupled with gradual liberalization of FDI policy as part of cautious capital account liberalization process and robust domestic economic performance has increased its attractiveness as a preferred destination for FDI inflows. Before analysing the trends of FDI inflows, it is to be noted that the definition of FDI in India has undergone changes in an attempt to bring it in line with international practices. Prior to 2000–01, FDI statistics compiled by the RBI in the Balance of Payments included only equity capital recorded under five heads: (i) Reserve Bank of India's automatic approval route for equity holdings up to 51 per cent; (ii) Foreign Investment Promotion Board or Secretariat of Industrial Approval's discretionary approval route for larger projects with equity holding greater than 51 per cent; (iii) acquisition of shares route since 1996 (relating to acquisition of shares of Indian companies by non-resident under Section 29 of FERA); (iv) RBI's non-resident Indian (NRI) schemes and (v) external commercial borrowings (American Depository Receipts, Global Depository Receipts and Euro equities). This definition differed from that of the IMF which includes external commercial borrowings, reinvested earnings and subordinated debt. This led to an underestimation of FDI inflows. Since 2000–01, the coverage of FDI was expanded and brought in line with the IMF definition. Besides equity capital, FDI now also covered reinvested earnings (retained earnings of FDI companies) and other direct investment capital (intra-company loans or intra-company debt transactions) (Mishra and Puri 2011; NCAER 2010–11). On this basis, it is not logical to compare the data since 2000–01 with the data prior to this year. Therefore after drawing the trends of FDI inflows in India since 1991 (Fig. 4.3), it was disaggregated into two sub periods, i.e. 1991/92–1999/2000 and 2000/01–2011/12 (Table 4.3)

A look at the trend of FDI inflows in India Fig. 4.3a shows that starting from a conservative approach towards foreign investment, India moved in favour of more liberalized policy stance from early 1990s onwards, inter alia in terms of wider access to different sectors of the economy, ease of starting business, repatriation of dividend and profits and relaxations regarding norms for owning equity. This progressive liberalization coupled with considerable improvement in terms of macroeconomic fundamentals was reflected in growing size of FDI flows into the country.[5]

Table 4.3 shows that during the first decade of the liberalization policy (i.e. 1991–2000), foreign investment in the country increased with a rate of 18 per cent. After updating the definition of FDI, since 2000–01, there was a manifold increase in inflows of foreign investment. The steep rise in FDI inflows (since 2004–05) has sustained even during the period of

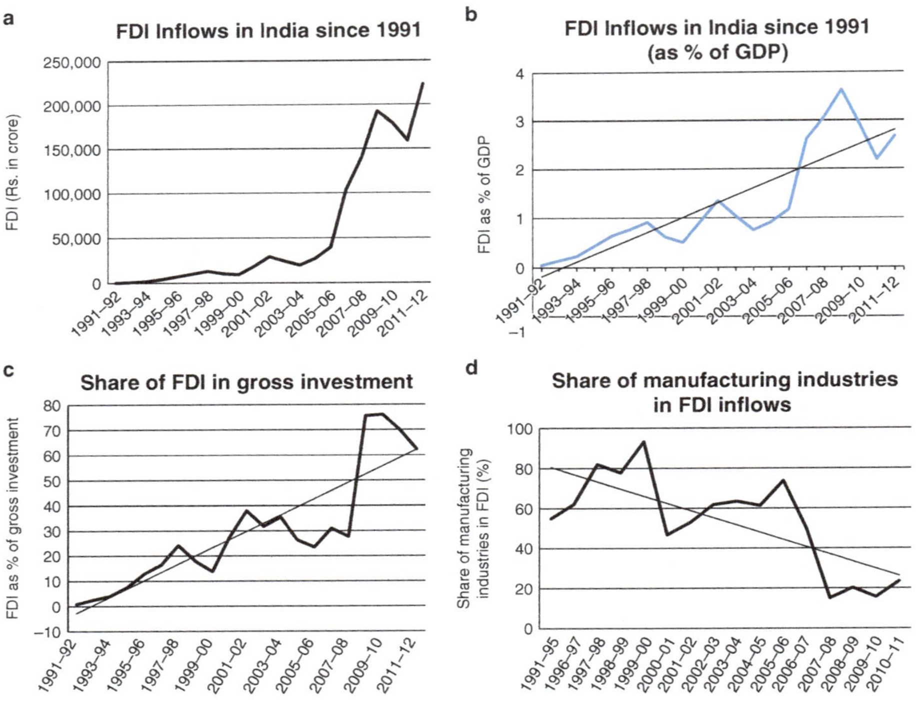

Fig. 4.3 (a) FDI inflows in India since 1991. *Source*: *Handbook of Statistics on Indian Economy*, 2012–13, RBI. (b) FDI inflows in India (as % of GDP) *Source*: *Handbook of Statistics on Indian Economy*, 2012–13, RBI and Economic Survey of India. (c) Share of FDI in gross investment. *Source*: Reserve Bank of India and Ministry of Commerce and Industry, Govt. of India, 2012–13. (d) Share of manufacturing industries in FDI inflows. *Source*: Compiled from the statistics released by SIA Newsletter Annual Issue, Ministry of Commerce & Industry, 2012–13

Table 4.3 Growth rates of indicators of FDI inflows

Indicators	*Year*	$Y_t = a + b_t$
Log (FDI)	1991/92–1999/2000	2.67 + 0.18t
	2000/01–2011/12	4.08 + 8.28t
Share of FDI in GDP	1991/92–1999/2000	0.06 + 0.08t
	2000/01–2011/12	0.52 + 0.21t
Share of FDI in gross investment	1991/92–1999/2000	−1.06 + 2.44t
	2000/01–2011/12	16.62 + 4.17t
Share of FDI in manufacturing	1991/92–1999/2000	46.34 + 9.23t
	2000/01–2011/12	71.19 − 4.25t

Note: Growth Rates are calculated by semi-log trend equation: $\log Y_t = a + b_t$

Source: Computed from *Handbook of Statistics on Indian Economy*, SIA Newsletter, Annual Issue, Ministry of Commerce and Industry, GOI, Economic Survey of India, 2012–13

global economic crisis with some moderation (2008–09 and 2009–10).[6] According to Reserve Bank of India, this reflected the continued strength of sustained economic activity and positive investment climate (with inflows channelling into financial, manufacturing and construction sectors). The strength of the corporate performance, positive investor sentiment, further liberalization of FDI policies in sectors such as telecom, retail, and expanding promotional efforts by the government also played a role in attracting FDI.[7]

However, when the global FDI flows to EMEs[8] recovered during 2010–11, FDI flows to India remained sluggish despite strong domestic growth ahead of global recovery (IMF, Balance of Payment Statistics). According to economists, policy makers, academicians and corporates and researchers, the divergent trends in FDI flows could be the result of certain institutional factors[9] that dampened the investors' sentiments for investing into India. On account of this, Government of India further liberalized its FDI policy on April, 2011 to promote FDI inflows to India. These measures, *inter alia* included (i) allowing issuance of equity shares against non-cash transactions such as import of capital goods under the approval route, (ii) removal of the condition of prior approval in case of existing joint ventures/technical collaborations in the 'same field', (iii) providing the flexibility to companies to prescribe a conversion formula subject to FEMA/SEBI guidelines instead of specifying the price of convertible instruments upfront, (iv) simplifying the procedures for classification into two categories – 'companies owned and controlled by foreign investors' and 'companies owned and controlled by Indian residents' and (v) allowing FDI in the development and production of seeds and planting material without the stipulation of 'under controlled conditions'. These measures were found to be favourable as the FDI inflows shot up during 2011–12 (Fig. 4.3a).

The share of FDI in GDP (Fig. 4.3b) has increased with an average rate of 0.21 per cent annually during the 2000s which is more than double the growth rate during the 1990s. The share of FDI in GDP reached the peak in 2008–09 after that there is a steep decline. The recovery in the share of FDI in GDP started from 2011 to 2012. The reasons for these fluctuations are explained earlier.

The share of FDI in gross investment (Fig. 4.3c) has shown almost the similar trend. The growth rate of share of FDI in gross investment has almost doubled in the 2000s as compared to the 1990s. Surprisingly, the share of manufacturing industries in FDI (Fig. 4.3d) has shown a decreasing trend. During the 1990s, it was increasing with an average rate of 9.23 per cent, and during the 2000s, it is decreasing with an average rate of 4.25 per cent. A perusal of the data on sectoral shares of FDI in India reveals the emergence of service sector, telecommunication, construction and hotel and tourism, over the two sub-periods. These sectors have a significance in contribution to country's economic growth on the one hand, and on the other, they play an important role in the growth of manufacturing industries and also the manufacturing exports. During January 2000 to November 2012, service sector have shared a maximum portion of FDI (20 per cent) in which dominating ones are financial sector (7.1 %) and non-financial/business services (6 %). The services like banking, insurance, and others share about 1 to 2 per cent of total FDI.[10] The service sector is followed by construction (12 %) and telecommunication (7 %).[11] It is to be mentioned here that as part of capital account liberalization, FDI was gradually allowed in almost all sectors, except a few on ground of strategic importance, subject to compliance of sector-specific rules and regulations.

FDI inflows into manufacturing industries have been computed based on the FDI records provided by DIPP. The share of top 20 industries receiving the highest amount of FDI inflows is presented in Table 4.4. During 1990–91 to 2000–01, among the top five recipients of FDI, transportation industry (10.2 %) was receiving the highest amount followed by electrical equipment (including S/W and electrical) (9.4 %), chemicals (other than fertilizer) (7.3 %), fuel (power and oil refinery) (6.6 %) and food processing industry (4.2 %). These industries together

Table 4.4 Top 20 manufacturing industries in terms of FDI inflows

Rank	*1990–91 to 2000–01*		*2000–01 to 2010–11*	
	Sector	*% share*	*Sector*	*% share*
1	Transportation industry	10.2	Electricals equipment (including software and electrical)	19.3
2	Electricals equipment (including software and electrical)	9.4	Metallurgical industries	10.5
3	Chemicals (other than fertilizers)	7.3	Chemicals (other than fertilizers)	7.5
4	Fuels (power and oil refinery)	6.6	Cement and gypsum products	6.0
5	Food processing industries	4.2	Transportation industry	5.6
6	Paper and pulp including paper product	1.8	Drugs and pharmaceuticals	4.9
7	Drugs and pharmaceuticals	1.7	Fuels (power and oil refinery)	4.6
8	Miscellaneous mechanical and engineering	1.5	Food processing industries	3.1
9	Textiles (include dyed, printed)	1.3	Textiles (include dyed, printed)	2.3
10	Glass	1.1	Miscellaneous mechanical and engineering	2.3
11	Metallurgical industries	1.1	Fermentation industries	1.5
12	Commercial, office and household equipment	1.0	Paper and pulp including paper Product	1.1
13	Cement and gypsum products	0.8	Ceramics	1.1
14	Industrial instruments	0.6	Machine tools	1.0
15	Rubber goods	0.5	Medical and surgical appliances	1.0
16	Agricultural machinery	0.3	Rubber goods	0.8
17	Ceramics	0.3	Commercial, office and household equipment	0.6
18	Machine tools	0.3	Vegetable oils and vanaspati	0.5
19	Fermentation industries	0.2	Soaps, cosmetics and toilet preparations	0.5
20	Leather, leather goods and pickers	0.2	Agricultural machinery	0.4
Total Share of Manufacturing Industries		69.59	Total share of manufacturing industries	28.73

Source: SIA Newsletter, Deptt. of Industrial Policy and Promotion, GoI, Ministry of Commerce and Industry, Jan 2005, Nov 2008 and Jan 2014

comprised about 38 per cent of the FDI inflows in manufacturing industry. Out of these industries, only three industries maintained their top five position during 2000–01 to 2010–11. These are electrical equipment (including S/W and Electrical) (19.3 %), chemicals (other than fertilizers) (7.5 %) and transportation industry (5.6 %). The other industries which were added in the category of top five industries are metallurgical industries (10.5 %) and cement and gypsum products (6 %). Fuels (power and oil refinery) (4.6 %) declined its position in receiving the FDI inflows. About eight industries received their share of foreign investment in the range of 1 to 3 per cent and the rest are below 1 per cent. During the sub-period 2000–01 to 2010–11, electrical equipment occupied the highest share followed by metallurgical industries, chemical (other than fertilizers), cement and gypsum products, transportation industry, drugs and pharmaceuticals and fuels (power and oil refinery) with their share being 19.3, 10.5, 7.5, 6.0, 5.6, 4.9 and 4.6 per cent respectively. The overall share of manufacturing industries during 1990/91 to 2000/01 was 70 per cent which decreased to 29 per cent during 2000/01 to 2010/11.

Further, an attempt is made to determine the sources of FDI inflows into India. Table 4.5 shows the share of top 10 countries investing in India for the two sub-periods, viz. 1991–2000 and 2000–2014. The highest share of FDI

Table 4.5 Share of top 10 investing countries

Rank	*January 1991 to December 2000*	*April 2000 to January 2014*
1	Mauritius (20.6)	Mauritius (37)
2	US (12.9)	Singapore (11)
3	Japan (4.6)	UK (10)
4	Germany (3.5)	Japan (7)
5	UK (3.3)	US (6)
6	Netherlands (3.3)	Netherland (6)
7	Korea (South) (2.9)	Cyprus (5)
8	Italy (2.0)	Germany (3)
9	Singapore (1.8)	France (3)
10	France (1.7)	UAE (2)
Total FDI inflows in India (Rs. in million)	702041.06	10103140
Total FDI inflows in manufacturing (Rs. in million)	532865.10 (75.9 %)	6250340 (61.9 %)

Source: Computed from FDI Statistics, DIPP, Jan 2014

is from Mauritius. Its share in FDI inflows was 21 per cent during the 1990s which increased to 37 per cent during the 2000s. This could be attributed to the double taxation treaty[12] that India has signed with Mauritius and also to the fact that most US investment into India is being routed through Mauritius (NCAER 2010–11). Singapore (11 %) is the second largest investor in India followed by UK (10 %), and other developed countries like Japan, US and Netherland. These countries are also the major trading partners of India. The significance of Korea (South) and Italy has declined in terms of top 10 industries investing in India. The share of Japan, UK, Netherland, Singapore and France has increased. Cyprus and UAE have entered the list of top 10 investing countries during the recent cumulative period.

4.4 Foreign Technology Transfers

The increase in FDI inflows in India is associated with foreign technology transfer approvals. After the liberalization of economic policy since 1991 to February 2009, a total of 8,049 technological collaboration are approved. India's increasing quest for advanced technology to modernize its industrial sector is evidenced from the sector-wise approvals for foreign technology

Table 4.6 Foreign technology collaboration (August 1991 to August 2010)

Sectors	*Total approvals (nos.)*	*Sectoral percentage*
Electrical equipment (including electronics and software)	1,263	15.5
Chemicals (other than fertilizers)	912	11.2
Industrial machinery	874	10.7
Transport industries (including automobiles)	761	9.4
Miscellaneous mechanical and engineering	444	5.5
Metallurgical industries	382	4.7
Fuels (including power and oil refineries)	411	5.1
Drugs and pharmaceuticals	276	3.4
Textiles	170	2.1
Food processing	166	2.0
Industrial instruments	121	1.5
Miscellaneous and other industries	1908	23.4
Total	8138	100

Source: DIPP Fact Sheet, April 2009

collaboration as shown in Table 4.6. During the period August 1991 to August 2010, out of the total technological collaborations, electrical equipment (including electronics and software) accounted for highest number of approvals (15.5 %) followed by chemicals (other than fertilizers) (11.2 %), Industrial machinery (10.7 %), transport industry (including automobiles) (9.4 %) and so on. According to the DIPP statistics, the majority of technology transfers have been from the US (23 %) followed by Germany (14 %), Japan (11 %) and UK (11 %).

4.5 India's International Trade Experiences (Since 1991)

On account of trade liberalization measures adopted in India since 1991, India's external trade has undergone significant changes in terms of trade and direction. Figure 4.4a reveals that in absolute terms, ignoring the period of global crisis (2008–09) and high oil prices (2009–10),[13] India's trade volume has continuously increased. The trend of total trade was somewhat flatter during the 1990s. From 1991 to 1999, India's international trade has almost doubled from $37 billion to $87 billion. Thereafter, during the 2000s, the trend has sharpened and increased by 10 folds till 2012. During the first decade of reforms period, the imports were slightly more than the exports. The difference increased during the second decade of the reforms and by 2012, the value of imports became almost 1.8 times the value of exports. India's share in the world trade (Fig. 4.4b) picked up during the 2000s and crossed the 2 per cent level in 2011. From 2008 onwards, the share of India's imports in the world's total imports has been greater than 2 per cent while the share of India's exports in world's total exports, though increasing, has not been able to cross the 2 per cent mark even today. India's share in world merchandise trade has shown almost the similar trend particularly during the 2000s (Fig. 4.4c). However, the results are surprising when the trend of India's share of manufacturing in merchandise trade is taken into consideration (Fig. 4.4d). Manufacturing exports have always dominated the India's merchandise exports, but the trend shows that this sector is gradually losing its shine. During the 1990s, the trend of the share of manufactures in merchandise exports and imports was almost stagnant.[14] The share of manufacturing exports varied in the range of 72 to 79 per cent while that of imports varied in the range of 49 to 54 per cent. However, during the 2000s, the share of both exports and imports in merchandise

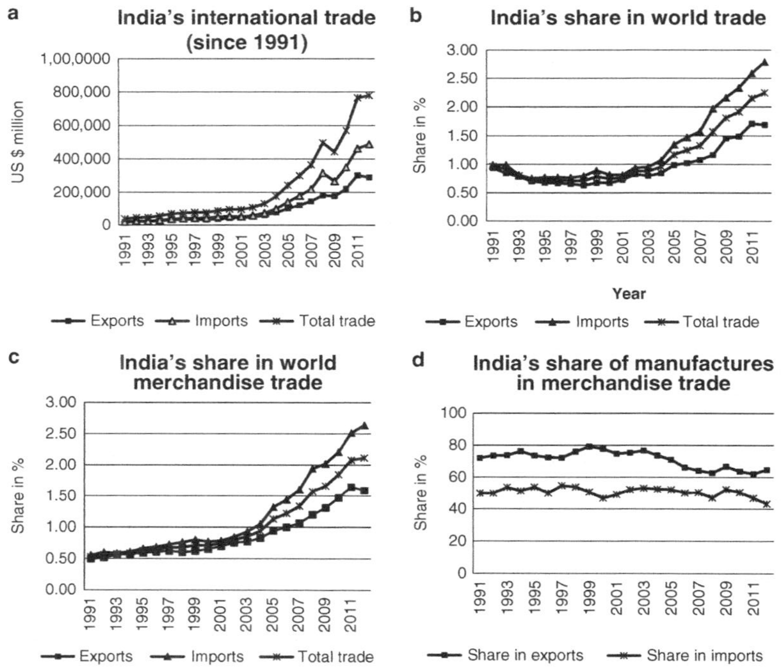

Fig. 4.4 (a) India's international trade (since 1991). (b) India's share in world trade. (c) India's share in world merchandise trade. (d) India's share of manufactures in merchandise trade *Source*: WITS Database, *UNCTAD Handbook of Statistics*, 2012, World Trade Organizations (WTO) Secretariat and IMF: Ministry of Commerce and Industry, Government of India (27 October 2011), Databook for DCH, Planning Commission, Government of India (10 March 2014)

trade has declined. The share of exports has declined from 78 per cent in 2000 to 65 per cent in 2012 and the share of imports has declined from 47 per cent in 2000 to 43 per cent in 2012. This might be due to petroleum products which share a significant portion of trade, but they are not included in the category of manufacturers.[15] The share of petroleum products is increasing continuously after the reforms (Annexure A 4.2). Kumar and Gupta (2008) have related the decline in share of manufacturing in merchandise exports with policy lacunae in identifying the country's competitive advantage, low value exports and relatively poor inflow of FDI especially in export-oriented units. It is also noteworthy that the share of manufacturing in merchandise exports has always been greater than that of imports, though this difference is declining.

The picture becomes clear when the composition of India's international trade is taken into account. With the liberalization of trade practices, the country is able to explore trade possibilities on the basis of comparative cost advantage. As a result, goods are traded at various stages of production. Also the transformation of economy from the controlled status to liberalized status results into transformation of the whole trade structure. Figure 4.5a,b reveals the composition of exports and imports by stages of processing, which is broadly disaggregated into consumer goods, intermediate goods, capital goods and raw materials. The figures are compared for the years 1990–91, 1997–98, 2004–05 and 2011–12. In exports, the share consumer goods and intermediate goods has witnessed a decline from 42 and 39 per cent in 1997–98 to 47 and 31 per cent in 2011–12. While the share of capital goods has increased from 6 per cent in 1997–98 to 12 per cent in 2012. The overall share of raw materials in exports has shown a decline from 14 per cent in 1990–91 to 9 per cent in 2011–12.

Regarding imports, the share of consumer goods has decreased from 15 per cent in 1990–91 to 10 per cent in 2011–12. Intermediate goods have increased its share from 27 per cent in 1990–91 to 35 per cent in 2011–12. The share of capital has increased till 2004–05 from 14 per cent to 20 per cent but thereafter, it declined to 16 per cent in 2011–12. The share of raw material in total imports has increased from 35.61 per cent in 1990–91 to 41.59 per cent in 2011–12.

The comparison of the Fig. 4.5a,b shows that in exports, the increase in the share of consumer goods is associated with decrease in the share of intermediate goods, capital goods and raw materials. On the other hand, in imports, the decrease in the share of consumer goods is associated with increase in the share of intermediate goods, capital goods and raw materials.

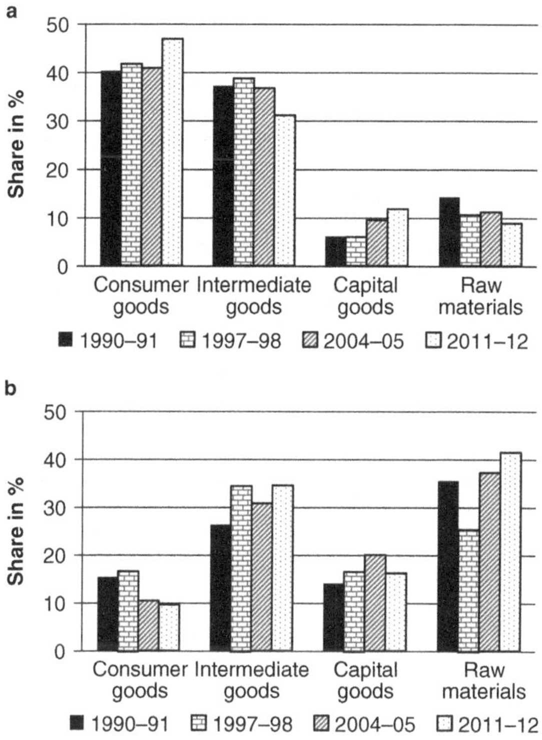

Fig. 4.5 India's international trade by stages of processing. (a) Exports by stages of processing. (b) Imports by stages of processing (*Source*: WITS Database)

This clearly shows that the trade-oriented liberalization process has driven the Indian economy towards the production of final goods for other economies under the broad framework of global production linkages.[16]

Further, the sector-specific composition of manufacturing exports and imports is compared for the years 1990–91, 1997–98, 2004–05, and 2011–12. The sectors are ranked according to their share in manufacturing exports and imports and only the top 10 sectors are shown in Table 4.7a and b. Since petroleum products has emerged as an important export item of the merchandise exports for India in recent years, the study has covered it in the category of manufacturing exports.[17] At the commodity level, petroleum products, occupying the first rank, are leading the India's merchandise

Table 4.7a Top 10 manufacturing exports (1990–91 to 2011–12) – commodity wise

Rank	*1990–91*	*1997–98*	*2004–05*	*2011–12*
1	Textile and textile products (23.93)	Textile and textile products (25.85)	Gems and jewellery (16.47)	Petroleum products (18.22)
2	Gems and jewellery (16.11)	Gems and jewellery (15.27)	Textile and textile products (16.23)	Gems and jewellery (15.4)
3	Chemicals and related products (9.52)	Chemicals and related products (15.24)	Chemicals and related products (14.9)	Chemicals and related products (12.21)
4	Leather and manufactures (7.99)	Leather and manufactures (12.56)	Petroleum products (8.37)	Textile and textile products (9.19)
5	Machinery and instruments (3.84)	Machinery and instruments (4.73)	Iron and steel (4.69)	Transport equipment (6.87)
6	Petroleum products (2.88)	Metals (3.42)	Machinery and instruments (4.45)	Machinery and instruments (4.72)
7	Metals (2.51)	Transport equipment (2.92)	Metals (4.07)	Metals (3.16)
8	Transport equipment (2.21)	Iron and steel (2.65)	Transport equipment (3.39)	Electronic goods (2.92)
9	Other engineering goods (1.67)	Electronic goods (2.5)	Leather and manufactures (2.9)	Other engineering goods (2.25)
10	Electronic goods (1.28)	Other engineering goods (2.17)	Electronic goods (2.19)	Iron and steel (2.12)

Note: Figures in parentheses show the share in total exports.

Source: World Integrated Trade Solution (WITS), Economic Survey, Various Issues

exports in 2011–12 with a share of 18 per cent. Gems and jewellery has maintained an impressive share (15 to 17 %) in the manufacturing exports with a second rank. Chemicals and related products have always maintained its third rank during the post-reforms period. Its share in exports has increased from below 10 per cent in 1990–91 to above 12 per cent in 2011–12. Chemical products covers a wide range of items from fine chemicals and pharmaceuticals to dyes and from plastics to rubber products.

While most of these items have done well, pharmaceutical products have shown the lead. Bulk drugs, intermediates, generics and formulations have all been the growth drivers. The textile sector, including apparel, which was the largest export sector and accounted for almost a quarter of our exports till late 1990s, has dipped to 16 per cent in 2004–05 and further to 9 per cent in 2011–12. The decline is severe in the case of cotton yarn, fabrics, made-ups, etc. and readymade garments. Their shares has declined from 9 per cent in 1997–98 and 12 per cent in 1990–91 to 2 per cent and 4.5 per cent in 2011–12 respectively. This is because of the dismantling of the textile quota regime in the developed markets from 01–01-2005 as per the WTO Agreement on Textiles and Clothing (ATC) (Taneja, n.d.). Engineering goods, at the individual levels, have occupied 5th to 10th rank among the top 10 category of manufacturing exports. The share of transport equipment, machinery and instruments, metals, electronic goods, other engineering goods and iron and steel are 7, 5, 3, 3, 2 and 2 per cent respectively. As a product group, engineering goods are capturing the maximum portion of exports, with a share of 22 per cent in 2011–12 (more than one-fifth of the total export earning). During 1990–91, its share in manufacturing exports was only 12 per cent. Among the exports of engineering goods, the share of transport equipment has gained importance during the past two decades. Its share has increased from 2 per cent in 1990–91 to 7 per cent in 2011–12. The share of electronic goods has also increased from a less than 1 per cent in 1990–91 to 3 per cent in 2011–12. Iron and steel gained importance as a foreign exchange earner till 2004–05 as its share in manufacturing exports was around 5 per cent, thereafter it dipped to 2 per cent in 2011–12. Machinery and instruments, though declined in rank from 3rd in 1990–91 to 6th in 2004–05, its share has increased from a less than four per cent in 1990–91 to 5 per cent in 2011–12. Other engineering goods have shown their fluctuating performance. After engineering goods, petroleum product is the second most important product group in merchandise exports. In 1991, its share was only 3 per cent. According to the Economic Survey (2007–08), 'the perceptible increase in the share of petroleum products in total exports reflected not only the rise in POL prices but also India's enhanced refined capacity'. Leather and manufactures, with a share of 8 per cent in manufacturing exports, was at 4th rank in 1990–91 and declined to 9th rank with a share of 3 per cent. In 2011–12, this product was away from the top 10 category of manufacturing exports.

In imports [Table 4.7b], crude and petroleum products have always attained the top position. Its share in total imports has galloped from

Table 4.7b Top 10 manufacturing imports (1990–91 to 2011–12) – commodity wise

Rank	*1990–91*	*1997–98*	*2004–05*	*2011–12*
1	Crude and petroleum products (14.28)	Crude and petroleum products (19.68)	Crude and petroleum products (26.76)	Crude and petroleum products (31.66)
2	Mainly export-related items (8.72)	Mainly export-related items (16.66)	Mainly export-related items (15.33)	Gold and silver (12.53)
3	Machinery except electrical and electronic (4.97)	Machinery except electrical and electronic (8.73)	Gold and silver (10)	Mainly export-related items (11.13)
4	Project goods (3.37)	Gold and silver (7.64)	Electronic goods (8.96)	Electronic goods (6.66)
5	Iron and steel (2.79)	Electronic goods (5.03)	Machinery except electrical and electronic (6.11)	Machinery except electrical and electronic (6.18)
6	Fertilizers (2.33)	Project goods (4.19)	Transport equipment (3.88)	Coal, coke, briquettes, etc. (3.56)
7	Electrical machinery except electronic (2.25)	Iron and steel (3.43)	Coal, coke and briquettes, etc. (2.87)	Transport equipment (2.87)
8	Transport equipment (2.2)	Coal, coke, briquettes, etc. (2.87)	Iron and steel (2.39)	Metalliferous ores, metal scrap, etc. (2.73)
9	Metalliferous ores, metal scrap, etc. (2.02)	Fertilizers (2.69)	Metalliferous ores, metal scrap, etc. (2.21)	Iron and steel (2.45)
10	Non-ferrous metals (1.45)	Transport equipment (2.53)	Professional, scientific controlling instruments, photographic optical goods (1.37)	Fertilizers (2.35)

Note: Figures in parentheses show the share in total imports

Source: World Integrated Trade Solution (WITS), Economic Survey, Various Issues

14 per cent in 1990–91 to 32 per cent in 2011–12. This increase in the share of import expenditure on crude and petroleum products is attributed to the increase in prices. Also, the demand of energy at the consumer as well as the manufacturing levels has considerably increased during the two decades. The dramatic increase in the prices of crude and petroleum products is one of the important components for increase in the import expenditure on raw materials and intermediate goods. Gold and silver has emerged as an important import item in 1997–98 with a share of 7 per cent. Thereafter, its share in import expenditure increased continuously and finally reached to 13 per cent in 2011–12, thus making it the second most important item of imports. Imports for the mainly export-related items have occupied the third rank with a share of 11 per cent. Among the export-related items, the important ones are pearls, precious and semi-precious stones whose import has increased due to the increase in the export demand of gems and jewellery. The share of pearls, precious and semi-precious stones was below 5 per cent in 1990–91 which increased to more than 6 per cent in 2011–12. Organic and inorganic chemicals is also one of the important item among imports for export-related items. In 2011–12, its share in total imports is found to be around 4 per cent. The top 10 positions attained by electronic goods, machinery except electrical and electronic and transport equipment with their shares being 7, 6 and 3 per cent respectively in 2011–12 are important in increasing the share of capital goods imports. The imports of coal, coke and briquettes has emerged in the top 10 category of manufacturing imports in 1997–98 with 8th rank. Increase in the demand for energy at the domestic level has increased its share in imports to around 4 per cent thus giving it the 6th rank in 2011–12. The share of metalliferous ores, metal scrap, etc. in total imports has significantly declined from 9 per cent in 1997–98 to 2 per cent in 2004–05 which marginally increased in 2011–12. Also the share of iron and steel has remained in the range of 2 to 3 per cent. Both these products along with fertilizers, crude and petroleum products, coal, coke and briquettes, metalliferous ores, metals, scraps, etc. comprises about two-fifths of the total imports and thus contributes significantly to the import of raw materials. The project goods, which were at 4th rank in 1990–91 were among the top 10 category till 1997–98, thereafter, they declined their importance.

Further, the liberalized policy regimes adopted in 1991 enabled India to explore the possibilities of developing trade relations with other countries

Table 4.8a India's top 10 export partners

1991	*1998*	*2005*	*2012*
US (16.35)	US (21.68)	US (16.48)	US (12.84)
Japan (9.24)	Hong Kong, China (5.66)	UAE (8.39)	UAE (12.36)
Soviet Union (9.18)	UAE (5.62)	China (7.16)	China (5.09)
Germany (7.11)	UK (5.59)	Singapore (5.41)	Singapore (4.68)
UK (6.37)	Germany (5.57)	UK (4.94)	Hong Kong, China (4.12)
UAE (4.13)	Japan (4.97)	Hong Kong, China (4.42)	Netherlands (3.27)
Belgium–Luxembourg (3.74)	Belgium–Luxembourg (3.89)	Germany (3.47)	Saudi Arabia (2.95)
Hong Kong, China (3.44)	Italy (3.18)	Belgium (2.78)	UK (2.8)
Italy (3.25)	Bangladesh (3)	Italy (2.52)	Germany (2.46)
France (2.38)	France (2.52)	Japan (2.45)	Japan (2.22)

Note: Figures in parentheses show the shares of the countries in India's total export

Source: World Integrated Trade Solution (WITS), Economic Survey, Various Issues

of the world. Thus new vistas for developing trade relations with other countries opened up. The development of bilateral, regional and multi-lateral trade relations has expanded the market for both exports and imports. Table 4.8a and b reveals the changes in the top importing and exporting partners for India after the trade reforms. On the export side (Table 4.8a), during the early years of reforms, out of the top 10 ranks, eight were acquired by the developed marketing economies (OECD nations). They were the US (16 %), Japan (9 %), Soviet Union (9 %), Germany (7 %), UK (6 %) and so on. As a whole, more than half of the India's exports were captured by the developed nations. However, over the two decades, the share of developed nations in India's exports declined as new economies joined as export partners. Although the US is still ranked the highest as export partner (13 %), UAE has reached the second position since 2005 with its share of 8 per cent and 12 per cent for 2005 and 2012 respectively. It appears that UAE is competing with the US as the difference between the shares of both countries in export is decreasing very rapidly and has now reached at par with a difference of less than half per cent. The emerging economies like China and Singapore have acquired the prominent position (3rd and 4th) as Indian export partners. The position

Table 4.8b India's top 10 import partners

1990	*1998*	*2005*	*2012*
US (10.28)	US (8.59)	China (7.29)	China (11.07)
Germany (8.03)	Switzerland (6.94)	US (6.34)	UAE (7.73)
Saudi Arabia (7.43)	Belgium–Luxembourg (6.79)	Switzerland (4.39)	Saudi Arabia (6.71)
Belgium (7.15)	UK (6.19)	Germany (4.04)	Switzerland (5.87)
Japan (7.05)	Japan (5.82)	Australia (3.32)	US (4.93)
UAE (6.43)	Germany (5.05)	Belgium (3.17)	Iraq (3.99)
UK (6.19)	Saudi Arabia (4.32)	South Korea (3.06)	Kuwait (3.64)
Russia (3.75)	UAE (4.06)	UAE (2.92)	Qatar (3.35)
Singapore (5.11)	Malaysia (3.79)	France (2.76)	Germany (3.02)
France (3.75)	Kuwait (3.54)	Japan (2.72)	Indonesia (2.88)

Note: Figures in parentheses show the shares of the countries in India's total imports

Source: World Integrated Trade Solution (WITS), Economic Survey, Various Issues

of Hong Kong in India's exports has improved (7th to 5th ranks) while that of Japan, Germany, Italy, France and Belgium have deteriorated. On account of this, the export earnings from Asian developing economies has increased considerably as their share in total exports has increased from 14 per cent in 1990–91 to 26 per cent (nearly one-fourth of total exports) in 2011–12.

On the import side [Table 4.8b], during 1991, more than half of the imports were shared by the OECD nations. The shares of these economies however declined with time. Due to increase in the domestic consumption of energy and rising fuel prices, the place of developed marketing economies was taken over by the group of oil exporting countries (OPEC). From a share of 16 per cent in 1990–91, the share of this group increased to nearly 40 per cent in 2012. Not only this, in 2012, the OPEC nations comprise the maximum ranks in the top 10 categories of import partners. Among the OPEC nations, UAE itself is sharing about 8 per cent of India's imports followed by Saudi Arabia (7 %), Iraq (4 %), Kuwait (4 %) and Qatar (3 %). Also, as trade policy expanded, many new economies emerged as trade partners over the years. Particularly the share of Asian developing countries increased considerably in India's imports. Their share in India's imports increased from 28 per cent in 1990–91 to nearly 50 per cent in 2012. In 2005, China with a share of 7 per cent, replaced US and reached the first position. During 2012, China was sharing 11.07 per cent of imports followed by UAE (8 %). The share of Germany has declined considerably from 8 per cent in 1990–91 to 3 per cent in 2012 while Japan and France occupying the 4th and 10th ranks in 1990–91, declined their status and are now out of the category of top 10 importing partners. On the other hand, the share of OPEC nations increased considerably in 2012.

4.6 India's Trade Liberalization and Economic Growth

Trade liberalization enables the country to compete with other countries. The resulting increase in competition at the domestic front directs the resources from less advantageous activity to more advantageous activity. The efficient allocation of resource enhances productivity. Since the manufacturing sector has strong inter-sectoral linkages, a growth in manufacturing sector should mean the growth of other sectors as well as the overall growth of the economy. Under the export-oriented growth model, reduction of trade barriers and FDI are the important tools for enhancing the export efficiency and strengthening the balance of payment position of the country. Table 4.9 presents the impact of trade-related indicators on India's economic growth. Economic growth is found to be strongly associated with all the trade-related variables. The elasticity coefficient shows that growth is highly responsive to the increase in FDI in the long run. In the short run, growth is highly responsive to exports. A 1 per cent increase in export volume increases the GNP by around 5 per cent per annum. Under the liberal trade regime, imports were liberalized to increase the exports of manufacturing industries. This includes import of

Table 4.9 Relationship between trade liberalization and India's economic growth

S. No.	*Function*	*Constant*	*Coefficient*	R2	*Elasticity coefficient*
1.	$GNP_t = f(\text{trade volume})_t$	973.08	1.07*	99.6	1.71
2.	$GNP_t = f(\text{export})_t$	944.14	3.13*	99.6	4.54
3.	$GNP_t = f(\text{import})_t$	985.97	1.65*	99.6	2.76
4.	$GNP_t = f(\text{FDI})_{t-2}$	1078.40	35.92*	97.9	99.81
5.	$GNP_t = f(\text{FDI})_{t-3}$	1148.98	33.93*	98	100.86

*Significant at 5 % level.

Source: Computed

capital, raw material and intermediates. The table shows that a 1 per cent increase in import increases the growth by around 3 per cent.

4.7 Conclusion

Trade liberalization policies that were focused on export orientation were initiated through tariff reduction in a phased manner. The tariffs rate declined sharply for those industries whose products have export demand in developed countries. The FDI, technologies and capital inflows were inclined towards the growth of these manufacturing industries. Such industries are minerals, machine and electricals, metals, chemicals and petroleum. India's trade relations with the developed countries signify this fact. Due to cheaper availability of capital, intermediates and raw materials from the world, India's status has changed from exporter of primary goods to the exporter of finished goods. During the recent decade (the 2000s), the increasing demand for energy and rising fuel prices have made OPEC nations the important trading partners of India.

Looking into India's growth experiences, trade liberalization has solved the problem of resource scarcity and provided India with new heights in terms of economic growth. Among the various trade-related indicators, exports, imports and FDI have contributed to India's economic growth. Among them, FDI's effects are stronger in the long run.

It is concluded that trade liberalization is the engine of India's economic growth. The inflow of capital, FDI and technologies associated with exposure to knowledge, skills, talents and ideas with the other countries produces lot of social and economic changes at the domestic level. The need is to understand those changes in terms of costs and benefits.

Notes

1. Topawala and Khandelwal (2010).
2. In the programme of macroeconomic stabilization, there are two fundamental objectives. The first objective is to pre-empt a collapse of the balance of payments situation in the short term and to reduce the current account deficit in the medium term. The second objective is to curb inflationary pressures and expectations in the short term and to reduce the rate of inflation as soon as possible thereafter. The principle instruments of stabilization are fiscal policy and monetary policy, which seek to reduce the level of

aggregate demand in the economy, and are often used in conjunction with a devaluation, which seeks to stem destabilizing expectations (Nayyar 2011).

3. In response to a macroeconomic crisis, stabilization is often combined with adjustment and reform. Such programmes of structural adjustment, based on policy reform advocated by the international financial institutions, are concerned with the supply side in an endeavour to raise the rate of growth of output. Structural reform seeks to shift resources: (a) from the non-traded goods sector to the traded goods sector and within the latter from import competing activities to export activities; and (b) from the government sector to the private sector. Apart from resource allocation, structural reform seeks to improve resource utilization by (a) increasing the degree of openness of the economy and (b) changing the structure of incentives and institutions, which would reduce the role of State intervention to rely more on the market forces, dismantle controls to rely more on prices, and wind down the public sector to rely more on the private sector (Nayyar 2011).

   It is also to be noted here that stabilization programmes were a part of an arrangement with the IMF and structural adjustment programmes were a part of arrangement with the World Bank. It is worth noting that it was not possible for a country to enter into a stabilization programme with the IMF unless it entered into a structural adjustment programme with the World Bank (Nayyar 2011). These prescriptions of IMF and World Bank are based on neoclassical economics which assumes competitive markets, profit-maximizing firms and rational consumers.
4. The guidelines were outlined in the Chelliah report of the Tax Reform Commission constituted in 1991 (Topavala and Khandelwal 2010).
5. Division of the International Trade and Finance, Department of Economic and Policy Research, Reserve Bank of India.
6. Division of the International Trade and Finance, Department of Economic and Policy Research, Reserve Bank of India.
7. Reserve Bank of India, Annual Report, 2007–08, Mumbai, 2008.
8. Emerging Market Economies; Argentina, Brazil, Chile, India, Indonesia, Mexico, South Africa and Thailand.
9. These institutional factors are explained in terms of procedural delays, complex rules and regulations related to land acquisition, legal requirements and environmental obligations (CRISIL Report 2011; FDI Survey by FICCI, December 2010; Economic and Political Weekly, October 16, 2010; China Daily, November 6, 2010).
10. SIA Newsletter, Annual Issue, 2012.
11. DIPP, GoI.
12. The India-Mauritius Double Taxation Avoidance Agreement (DTAA) was signed in 1982. According to DTAA between India and Mauritius, capital gains arising from the sale of shares are taxable in the country of residence of

the shareholder and not in the country of residence of the Company whose shares have been sold. Therefore, a Company resident in Mauritius selling shares of an Indian company will not pay tax in India. Since there is no capital gains tax in Mauritius, the gain will escape tax altogether.

13. This period is pronounced by trade contraction in India.
14. Also see Kumar and Gupta (2008).
15. Also noted in Nayak et al. (2013).
16. As particular parts of a manufacturing process were separated out and located in different countries to take advantage of differences in labour and other costs, trade in intermediate goods grew rapidly (Ghose 2008). In theory, increased capital flows should have led to a substantial transfer of capital from developed countries, where it is abundant and hence earns low return, to developing countries, where it is scare and hence should bear high return (Ghose 2008).
17. The trade statistics treats petroleum products separately from manufacturing goods (Economic Surveys, all issue).

References

Agarwal, R N, and B Goldar. (1995): "Economic Reforms and Employment in India: Projections for the Year 2001-02", *Indian Journal of Labour Economics*, Vol. 38(4).

Bhattacharyya, Rajib. (2012): "The Opportunities and Challenges of FDI in Retail in India", *IOSR Journal of Humanities and Social Sciences*, Vol. 5(5), Nov.–Dec.

Cerra, Valerie, and Sweta Chaman Saxena. (2000), "What Caused the 1991 Currency Crisis in India?" *International Monetary Fund Working Paper 00/157*, IMF.

Chand, Satish, and Kunal Sen. (2002): "Trade Liberalization and Productivity Growth: Evidence from Indian Manufacturing", *Review of Development Economics*, Vol. 6(1).

China Daily, November 6, 2010, weblink: www.chinadaily.com, accessed on 24-12-2013.

Chopra, Ajai, Charles Collyns, Richard Hemming, and Karen Parker (1995): "India: Economic Reform and Growth", *IMF Occasional Paper No. 134.*

CRISIL Report (2011), weblink: www.crisil.com, accessed on 12-03-2013.

Das, D.K., (2003): "Manufacturing Productivity under Varying Trade Regime: India in the 1980s and 1990s", *Working Paper 107*, ICRIER, New Delhi.

Databook for DCH, Planning Commission, Government of India (10th March, 2014), weblink: http://www.planningcommission.gov.in/data/datatable/1203/databook_1203.pdf

Department of Industrial Policy and Promotion (DIPP), Government of India, Ministry of Commerce and Industry, weblink: www.dipp.nic.in

Division of the International Trade and Finance, Department of Economic and Policy Research, Reserve Bank of India.

Economic and Political Weekly, October 16, 2010.

Economic Survey (2007–08): Ministry of Finance, Government of India.

Economic Survey (various issues), Government of India, weblink: indiabudget.nic.in/survey.asp

FDI Survey by FICCI, December 2010, weblink: ficci.in/Sedocument/20097/FICCI_FDI_Survey_Dec_2010.pdf, accessed on 18-06-2013.

Ghose, Ajit K. (2008): "Globalisation and Employment in Developing Countries", *Indian Journal of Labour Economics*, Vol. 51(4).

Ghosh, Jayati. (2006): "Trade Liberalisation and Economic Restructuring: Can India skip the Industrial Phase?", *Paper for IDEAs Conference on Post Liberalisation Constraints on Macroeconomic Policies*, Muttukadu, 27–29 January.

Goldar, Bishwanath. (2002): "Trade Liberalization and Manufacturing Employment: The Case of India", *International Labor Organization Employment Paper 2002/34.*

Handbook of Statistics on Indian Economy, Reserve Bank of India, weblink: https://rbidocs.rbi.org.in/.

Hasan, Rana, Devashish Mitra, and K. V. Ramaswamy. (2003): "Trade Reforms, Labor Regulations and Labor Demand Elasticities: Evidence from India", *NBER Working Paper No. 9879*, Cambridge, MA: National Bureau of Economic Research, August.

IMF, Balance of Payment Statistics, weblink: http://www.imf.org/external/pubs/cat/longres.aspx?sk=19299

Krishna, Pravin, and Devashish Mitra. (1998): "Trade Liberalisation, Market Discipline and Productivity Growth: New Evidence from India", *Journal of Development Economics*, Vol. 56(2), 4.

Kumar, R., and A.S. Gupta (2008): "Towards a Competitive Manufacturing Sector", *Working Paper No. 203*, Indian Council for Research on International Economic Relations.

Ministry of Commerce and Industry, Government of India (27th October 2011),

Mishra, S.K., and V.K. Puri. (2011): *Economics of Development and Planning: Theory and Practice*, Himalaya Publishing House.

Nayak, Shibananda, Vani Aggarwal, and Preeti Mann (2013): "India's Manufacturing Exports Dynamics: An Analysis of Technology Intensity Transition", *Working Paper CWS/WP/200/6*, Centre for WTO Studies, Indian Institute of Foreign Trade, New Delhi, March.

Nayyar, Deepak. (2011): *Liberalization and Development*, Oxford University Press.

NCAER. 2010–11, weblink: http://www.ncaer.org/data.php

SIA Newsletter (various issues), Deptt. of Industrial Policy and Promotion, GoI, Ministry of Commerce and Industry, Jan 2005, Nov 2008 and Jan 2014.

Taneja, Rashmi. (n.d.): "Indian Textile Exports: Past and Present", *International Journal in Multidisciplinary and Academic Research*, Vol. 2(2),March-April, weblink: http://ssijmar.in/vol2no2/vol2no2.22.pdf, accessed on 12-10-2014.

Topavala, P., and A. Khandelwal. (2010): "Trade Liberalization and Firm Productivity: The Case of India", *The Review of Economics and Statistics, January*.

Trade Policy Review India (TPRI), 2010–11, World Trade Organization.

UNCTAD *Handbook of Statistics*, 2012.

Veermani, Arvind. (2012): Accelerating and Sustaining Growth: Economic and Political Lessons, *IMF Working Paper WP/12/185*, July.

WITS COMTRADE Database, http://wits.worldbank.org/wits/.

WTO Secretariat Solution.

CHAPTER 5

Changing Structure of Indian Manufacturing Industries

Abstract The structure of manufacturing industries depends upon the nation's industrial and trade policies and accessibility to resources, capital and technologies. The economic openness has enabled the developing countries to explore cheaper inputs and technologies and exchange knowledge and ideas across the world. This chapter focuses on the structural changes that have taken place in Indian manufacturing industries as a result of trade openness. The chapter deals with examining the overall changes in the growth pattern of manufacturing industries, determining structural changes at industrial level, comparing the trade liberalization, trade orientation and comparative advantage of Indian manufacturing industries and, finally, developing relationship between various trade-related variables like tariff rate, FDI, capital–labour ratio, import penetration, export orientation, revealed comparative advantage and technological intensity.

Keywords Structure changes · Trade orientation · Comparative advantage

The structure of manufacturing industries depends upon the industrial policies, trade policies, accessibility to resources, capital and technologies. During the past two decades, the economies of the world are converging due to relaxation of industrial licensing (licence raj),[1] liberalization of trade barriers and deregulation of financial markets. This has allowed the countries, especially the developing countries, to explore sources of cheaper

H. Jain, *Trade Liberalisation, Economic Growth and Environmental Externalities*, DOI 10.1007/978-981-10-2887-8_5

inputs and technologies across the world.[2] Also the developed countries, for low-cost labour and market, are shifting their industries to developing countries. This led to development of intra-industry production linkages. The integration of economies enables the countries to exchange knowledge and ideas, resulting into change in the structure and pattern of productivity.

The established theories, like Heckscher–Ohlin, predicts that because of the relative comparative advantages of developing countries in labour-intensive commodities, trade liberalization will trigger a specialization in domestic labour-intensive technologies and lead to the expansion of employment and output. Accordingly, trade liberalization in India was expected to shift its industrial structure towards labour-intensive industries by encouraging more labour-intensive methods of production in which India was expected to have a comparative advantage. The cheap labour was expected to help Indian manufacturing exporters to become price competitive (Das and Kalita 2009). These standard trade theories of general equilibrium were based upon extremely restrictive assumptions such as perfect competition, perfect labour, capital mobility and fixed technology. These assumptions themselves loose their significance in the presence of market imperfections.

On the other hand, the stylized trade theories are more close to the real world. These theories accept that trade changes the existing production technology through different channels. It is not always true that technology is exogenously given for a country. A country's technological orientation in production may change due to diminishing trade protectionism and increasing international trade (Wood 1994, 1997). This trade-induced technological change is mostly skilled labour biased, i.e., trade-induced skill-biased technological change demands more skilled labour replacing the unskilled labour (Sadhukhan n.d.). Developing countries augment their existing technology with advanced technology which is available cheaply through trade liberalization and increasing capital flows.

The globalization, i.e., the outward orientation of the economy is based upon competitive and efficiency-driven exports. In order to respond to competition and dynamic market forces, the gains from trade in developing countries are looked in terms of increasing the manufacturing output through import of cheaper raw material, intermediates, capital and technology accompanied with FDI and growth of MNCs. Also, significant developments in the field of technology, knowledge dissemination and transportation have aided an arrangement (Sunder 2012) of international outsourcing of production activities via global production network (GPN).

Through GPN, the countries take the advantage of differences in labour and other costs. Hummels et al. (2001) suggested that modest decline in trade costs can lead to large increase in volume of trade by encouraging vertical specialization, i.e., the breakup of production into geographically separate states in terms of outsourcing or global production sharing. According to Nathan and Posthuma (2009), international outsourcing of goods and services constitutes roughly one-third of global trade. Increased trade in goods and services, technology and knowledge as well as relocation of production sites in the global value chains changes the relative demand of factors (Roy 2008) in domestic industries. As the intra-industry openness increases, the structure of manufacturing industries changes. The resulting change in the country's pattern of specialization changes the revealed comparative advantage.

This chapter focuses on the structural changes that have taken place in Indian manufacturing industries as a result of trade openness. Section 5.1 examines the overall changes in growth pattern of manufacturing industries. Section 5.2 determines the structural changes at industry level. Section 5.3 compares the trade liberalization, trade orientation and comparative advantage of Indian manufacturing industries. Section 5.4 develops relationship between the various trade-related variables like tariff rate, FDI, capital–labour ratio, import penetration, export orientation, revealed comparative advantage and technology intensity. Section 5.5 concludes the chapter.

5.1 Growth Pattern of Indian Manufacturing Industries in the Liberalized Era

During the last two decades or so, the world trade pattern has changed remarkably as the developing countries are exporting a major part of the manufacturing goods to the developed world. These exports are heavily dependent upon the imports (at different phases of production), finances and technology. In a way, the global production linkages have enabled the industries in developing countries to overcome their resource constraints. This has changed the long-standing growth pattern of regulated system. Table 5.1 reveals the trade openness and growth structure of Indian manufacturing industries after liberalization. The trade openness is determined in terms of import intensity, export intensity, trade intensity and trade volume of manufacturing industries. The figures show that the imports which were nearly one-tenth of the total manufacturing output, during the beginning of economic reforms (1991–92), crossed

Table 5.1 Trade openness and growth structure of manufacturing industries

Year	*Indicators of trade openness*				*Structural indicators*			
	Import intensity	*Export intensity*	*Trade intensity*	*Trade volume (Rs. in thousand crores)*	*Capital–labour ratio (Rs. in lakh)*	*FDI (Rs. in thousand crores)*	*Share of high tech. industries in GVA*	*Value added per worker (Rs.in lakh)*
1991–92	0.12	0.16	0.28	55.61	1.8	7.93*	34.30	0.80
1992–93	0.15	0.19	0.35	71.06	2.2		35.93	0.97
1993–94	0.18	0.23	0.41	90.60	2.5		34.37	1.19
1994–95	0.19	0.26	0.44	109.18	3.0		34.41	1.38
1995–96	0.23	0.28	0.51	144.19	3.4		35.90	1.59
1996–97	0.22	0.28	0.50	155.42	4.0	6.22	35.01	1.94
1997–98	0.27	0.30	0.57	178.35	4.2	10.83	36.16	1.91
1998–99	0.30	0.33	0.63	202.30	4.6	8.06	43.64	2.15
1999–2000	0.32	0.37	0.70	235.41	4.9	8.71	43.05	2.31
2000–01	0.30	0.44	0.73	266.39	5.0	8.59	40.86	2.23
2001–02	0.32	0.42	0.75	276.70	5.6	15.48	41.10	2.36
2002–03	0.39	0.48	0.87	347.13	5.6	15.09	38.69	2.70
2003–04	0.45	0.53	0.99	416.13	6.0	12.59	38.33	3.15
2004–05	0.58	0.61	1.19	539.67	6.1	16.54	36.52	3.66
2005–06	0.69	0.65	1.34	669.04	6.7	29.12	38.66	4.00
2006–07	0.74	0.66	1.40	800.71	6.9	50.95	35.33	4.46
2007–08	0.81	0.67	1.48	931.37	8.1	21.04	33.31	5.29

2008–09	0.99	0.80	1.79	1174.36	9.3	38.61	35.94	5.40
2009–10	0.98	0.77	1.75	1279.04	11.5	24.73	37.54	5.91
2010–11	1.06	0.91	1.97	1579.72	12.7	31.06	36.13	6.50
2011–12	1.34	1.11	2.45	2633.19	14.5	–	–	7.27
2012–13	1.39	1.27	2.66	3535.20	–	–	–	–

Note:
(1) The figures are in real terms (deflated by wholesale price index, 100 = 2004–05)
(2) The figures represent only the manufacturing industries
(3) *The figures are for the period 1991–95
(4) Import intensity, export intensity and trade intensity are measured as percentage of their respective share in manufacturing output

Source:
(1) Annual Survey of Industries, Summary Results for Factory Sector
(2) DGCIS, Ministry of Commerce and Industry, Government of India
(3) *Handbook of Statistics on Indian Economy*, RBI, 2012–13

the mark of 100 per cent in 2010–11, though there were slight fluctuations particularly during the years 1996–97, 2000–01 and 2009–10. Export intensity reflects the outward orientation of the economy. The manufacturing exports which were not even sharing 20th part of total manufacturing output in 1991–92 has witnessed many times increase and has now crossed a figure of 90 per cent of manufacturing output. Fluctuations are visible in the figures of export intensity during the years similar to import intensity. A closer look at the figures of import intensity and export intensity indicates that till 2004–05, the export intensity was greater than the import intensity. However, from 2005 to 2006 onwards, import intensity became steeper in manufacturing industries while export intensity suffered a setback. This might be due to global slowdown which recovered during the subsequent years. The increase in import intensity and export intensity is reflected in trade intensity and trade volume. The manufacturing trade intensity, which was slightly greater than one quarter of GDP (0.28) in 1991 reached approximately 2 per cent of manufacturing output in 2010–11. Since the trade intensity suffers from endogeneity problem (Lee et al. 2004; Paul and Das 2012), trade volume is also calculated. The sustained increase in the trade volume reflects increased openness. As compared to 1991–92, the trade volume quadrupled in 1999–2000, which further increased by 6.5 times in 2010–11. The higher value of import intensity as compared to export intensity (after 2005–06), on the one hand, indicates deficit in the manufacturing trade, and on the other hand, it reflects that the value addition in the import goods for exports is not taking place in a desired manner. This reflects the inefficient utilization of resources. It may be due to increase in prices of import goods, existence of low-level technologies or lack of skill.[3] The decrease in share of FDI to manufacturing industries particularly from 2005 to 2006 could also be one of the reasons, as the foreign investment is now diverted for the development of other supporting sectors like infrastructure and information and technology. The widening gap between the two ratios during the recent decade is the matter of concern.

Table 5.1 further shows the trends of structural indicators of manufacturing industries. The indicators which can be easily quantifiable, and for which the time series data are readily available, are taken into consideration. These indicators are capital–labour ratio, FDI, share of high-technology industries in GVA and value added per worker. During the two decades of economic reforms, the capital–labour ratio has increased by about seven times. From a single-digit figure of 1.8 in 1991–92, the capital–labour ratio reached double digit in 2009–10 and, finally, attained a value of 12.7 in 2010–11.[4] This indicates the impressive inflow of capital in the manufacturing industries during the post-liberalized period. This also indicates that the ease in availability of capital has led the market-oriented manufacturing industries to adopt labour-displacing or capital-deepening production technology. This is justified from the figures of FDI in manufacturing sector. During 1991–95, FDI in manufacturing sector was around Rs. 8,000 crores, which increased by four times to around Rs. 31,000 crores till 2010–11. The inflow of capital and finances increases the productivity of resources in the host country, which otherwise remain idle under the resource scarcity circumstances. However, the share of high-technology industries in GVA is representing a somewhat different situation. In the open trade regime, when Indian industries have the opportunity to explore highly sophisticated value adding technologies in the world, the share of high-technology industries in GVA has declined during the recent decade. It has increased from 34 per cent in 1991–92 to 43 per cent in 1999–2000, but after that it has declined continuously and reached a lower figure of 36 per cent in 2010–11 (declined by 7 per cent). Value added per worker is an indication of the efficiency of technology as well as that of worker. It is revealed from the table that the value added per worker has continuously increased from a low value of Rs. 0.80 lakh in 1991–92 to a high value of 7.27 lakh in 2010–11.

In order to have a comparative picture of the post-liberalized growth pattern of Indian manufacturing industries, the growth rates of the indicators of trade openness and structural indicators of manufacturing industries is calculated by disaggregating the post-reform period into the 1990s (1990–91/1999–2000) and the 2000s (2000–01/2010–11). As shown in Table 5.2, all the indicators of trade openness have shown a higher growth rate in the later period (the 2000s) except export intensity. The growth rate of manufacturing exports has suffered due to global meltdown. The growth rate of import intensity is greater than the export intensity in both the periods.

As a whole, the comparison of the indicators of trade openness for the two periods indicated an increase in the degree of openness in the later period. The growth rate of trade volume has increased from 7.7 per cent during the 1990s to 8.2 per cent during the 2000s. Among the structural indicators of manufacturing, the growth rate of capital–labour ratio has witnessed a decline from 5.5 per cent growth rate during the 1990s to 3.9 per cent during the 2000s. The growth rate of FDI in manufacturing has

Table 5.2 Disaggregation of growth rates of trade openness and manufacturing growth structure

Indicators	*Growth rates*		
	1991–92/1999–2000	*2000–01/2010–11*	*Overall*
Import intensity	0.050	0.059	0.049
Export intensity	0.041	0.032	0.037
Trade intensity	0.041	0.045	0.043
Trade volume	0.077	0.082	0.073
Capital–labour ratio	0.055	0.039	0.037
FDI in manufacturing	0.096	0.052	0.078
Share of high-technology industries in GVA	0.012	-0.006	0.001
Value added per worker	0.06	0.05	0.04

Note: Growth rates are calculated by semi-log trend equation: $\log Y_t = a + bt$

Source: Author's calculation based on Table 5.1

declined from 9.6 per cent during the 1990s to 5.2 per cent during the 2000s. During the 1990s, the share of high-technology industries in GVA has increased with a rate of 1.2 per cent. It faced a severe decline during the 2000s. Its share has decreased with a rate of 0.6 per cent. The situation is not commensurate with the growth path achieved by Indian economy during 2000.[5] The rate of growth of value added per worker has slightly declined in the 2000s by 0.1 per cent. The higher inflow of FDI and capital from abroad indicates the inflow of skill-biased technology. However, on comparing the growth rate of value added per worker with that of capital–labour ratio, one can find that the value added by a unit of labour is much less as compared to the capital invested on each unit of labour. This reflects the lower efficiency of labour to work with imported capital, resulting into lower marginal productivity of capital.

5.2 Structural Changes at Industry Level

The inflow of capital, FDI as well as technology via trade liberalization has a major impact on the structure of domestic industries. Due to inter-industry dependency, the structural change in one industry influences the structure of other industries. Table 5.3 shows the structural changes within manufacturing industries in terms of capital–labour ratio, FDI per

Table 5.3 Industry-wise structural changes (in per cent) (1991–92/1999–2000 and 2000–01/2011–12)

NIC 2008	*Industry*	*1991–92/1999–2000*			*2000–01/2011–12*			*Technological intensity*
		K/L ratio (% change)	*FDI per year (amount in $ million)*	*Value added per worker (% change)*	*K/L ratio (% change)*	*FDI per year (amount in $ million)*	*Value added per worker (% change)*	
10	Food products	113.99	2456.90	64.19	76.93	1755.32	60.65	LT
11	Beverages	237.80	260.75	141.45	16.85	1992.47	20.86	LT
12	Tobacco products	209.72	–	115.64	42.17	–	37.77	LT
13–14	Textiles	238.60	2627.59	38.09	13.77	3094.71	-4.86	LT
15	Leather-related products	110.10	354.90	47.27	-17.08	167.49	-17.76	LT
16	Wood products (except furniture)	146.51	0.00	66.23	141.64	470.47	78.15	LT
17	Paper and paper products	141.65	2543.54	11.07	1.46	1565.01	33.71	LT
19	Coke and refined petroleum products	164.90	10491.84	43.03	161.94	7807.49	225.66	MLT
20–21	Chemicals and chemical products (including pharmaceuticals)	116.1	4647.12	98.19	16.7	8810.7	43.40	MHT
22	Rubber and plastic products	212.57	896.13	110.87	9.12	1095.07	3.08	MLT
23	Non-metallic minerals	143.51	926.10	10.33	-17.51	3316.06	29.37	MLT
24–25	Metals	60.4	1892.6	78.62	75.23	13306.77	79.30	MLT

(*continued*)

Table 5.3 (continued)

NIC 2008	*Industry*	*1991–92/1999–2000*			*2000–01/2011–12*			*Technological intensity*
		K/L ratio (% change)	*FDI per year (amount in $ million)*	*Value added per worker (% change)*	*K/L ratio (% change)*	*FDI per year (amount in $ million)*	*Value added per worker (% change)*	
26	Computer, electronic and optical products	96.08	44.58	68.26	12.71	59.61	21.88	HT
27–28	Electrical equipment	225.97	13840.46	51.23	50.84	29037.04	61.27	MHT
29–30	Transportation	535.66	7319.31	184.04	-24.84	4924.17	33.27	MHT
32	Other manufacturing	164.15	242.73	140.29	28.15	1335.69	-11.03	LT

Note: (1) K/L: Capita-labour ratio, HT: high technology, MHT: medium high technology, MLT: medium low technology, LT: low technology
(2) The classification of industries is based on the technological classification of Organisation for Economic Co-operation and Development (OECD, 2005), which relates R&D expenditure to value added and production statistics
(3) The classification of manufacturing industries according to technology group is given in Annexure (A 5.1)
Source: Classified by NCAER using DIPP data

year and technological intensity. During the 1990s, all the industries have witnessed an increase in capital–labour ratio. The increase is found to be highest for transportation (29–30) followed by textile (13–14), beverages (11), electrical equipment (27–28), rubber and plastic products (22) and tobacco (12). Among them, transportation and electrical equipment has a medium high-technology intensity, and textiles, beverages and tobacco have a low-technological intensity. During the 2000s, the increase in capital–labour ratio has slowed down for all the industries expect basic metals. For some industries, the percentage change in capital–labour ratio has shown a negative trend. These are transportation, non-metallic minerals and leather and related products. Comparing the growth of capital–labour ratio for all the industries in the 2000s, it is found to be highest for coke and refined petroleum products (19) followed by wood products (16), food products (10), metals (24–25) and electrical equipment (27). Out of them, only electrical equipment has medium high-technology intensity, while coke and refined petroleum products have medium low-technology intensity, and wood and food products have low-technology intensity. In regard to FDI, during the 1990s, electrical equipment (27–28), coke and refined petroleum products (19), transportation (29–30), chemicals (20–21), textiles (13) and paper and paper products (17) were found to be the important sectors. During the 2000s, electrical equipment (27–28) maintained its top position. Metals emerged as the second highest important industry for FDI. The other important industries are chemicals and chemical products (20–21), coke and refined petroleum products (19), transportation (29), non-metallic minerals (23) and textiles (13). Among them, electrical equipment, chemicals and chemical products and transportation are the medium high-technology industries. Metals and non-metallic minerals are medium low-technology industries. During 1990, change in value added per worker was positively highest for transportation followed by other manufacturing, tobacco and rubber and plastic products. The scenario changed in the 2000s. Now it is found to be highest for coke and refined petroleum products which is a medium low-technology industry. On comparing the percentage change in value added per worker during the 2000s with that of the 1990s, it is found to have remarkably increased for coke and petroleum products. This industry has achieved pre-eminent position in exports. For the other industries, the change in value added per worker is either slightly positive or highly negative.

As a whole, it can be said that high technology is adopted for the sectors which, on the one hand, can accelerate the growth of other sectors and, on

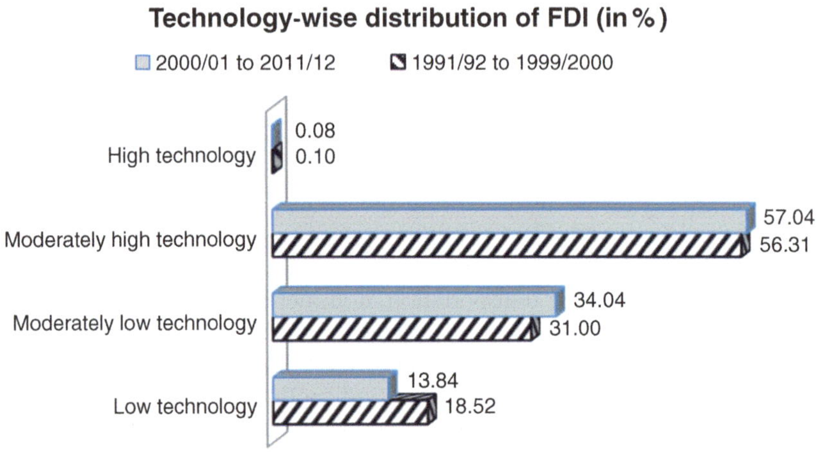

Fig. 5.1 Technology-wise distribution of FDI (in %) *Source:* Calculated from Table 5.3

the other hand, which is most important is that these sectors eases the marketing network and flows of finished goods to the developed (home) countries. These industries are chemicals and chemical products, computer, electronic and optical products, electrical equipment and transportation. The technology distribution of FDI in Fig. 5.1 reveals that medium high-technology-based industries have received more than half of the FDI after the reforms. It is followed by medium low-technology industries. These two technology groups have also shown an increase in receiving FDI during the 2000s as compared to the 1990s while low-technology industries have shown a decrease. The share of FDI in high-technology-based industries is even less than 1 per cent.

5.3 Trade Liberalization, Trade Orientation and Comparative Advantage

Further, trade liberalization through inflows of capital, intermediates and technology affects the economy both at the external and domestic fronts. The cheaper availability of inputs alters the comparative advantage of the domestic industries. Table 5.4 presents a scenario of trade liberalization,

Table 5.4 Tariff rate, trade orientation and comparative advantage

Industry	*1991–92/1999–2000*					*1999–2000/2011–12*				
	Tariff (% change)	*Import penetration (% change)*	*Export penetration (% change)*	*RCA (average)*	*GVA (% change)*	*Tariff (% change)*	*Import penetration (% change)*	*Export orientation (% change)*	*RCA (average)*	*GVA (% change)*
Food	-66.62	36.49	47.62	1.81	121.47	-10.11	63.6	92.62	1.38	205.27
Textiles	-56.55	-4.14	-233.53	4.08	746.31	-18.88	29.34	137.29	3.55	105.23
Leather	-54.16	-7.81	-175.65	3.25	673.44	-23.1	8.95	-5.07	2.37	193.33
Wood	-47.19	1034.85	193.13	0.14	-69.23	-20.86	185.17	77.34	0.24	332.86
Fuel	-22.5	694.83	52.56	0.20	117.46	-16.14	37.66	309.86	0.62	715.33
Chemicals (including pharmaceuticals)	-41.78	3.58	17.41	0.91	201.1	-25.4	119.7	82.99	1.23	136.89
Rubber and plastic	-67.97	35.35	42.58	0.37	-29.56	-26.88	129.62	77.8	0.64	233.72
Non-metallic	-46.85	2960.59	1910.06	5.86	408.32	-23.2	5088.42	18.56	5.73	1635.02
Metal	-56.03	-9.23	17.94	2.84	252.26	-25.5	33.13	13.64	2.91	454.67
Machine and electricals	-51.02	26.21	5.87	0.19	344.56	-20.46	129.69	42.02	0.32	335.67
Transportation	-23.54	6.61	-2.8	0.19	331.21	-17.05	37.74	98.67	0.34	285.43
Petroleum	-57.71	1.78	1012.75	1.17	110.70	-47.13	2.04	13488.24	6.97	4875.93

Note: (1) Import competition faced by an industry is measured using import penetration rate. It is an industry-level variable. The import penetration rate of *j*th industry in *i*th year is defined as $IPR_{jt} = Import_{jt} / (Output_{jt} + Import_{jt} - Export_{jt})$, where export and output respectively denote the export and output of industry *j* and import refers to the import of *j*th industry's product
(2) Export orientation is calculated as exports of industry *j*/output of industry *j*
(3) RCA provides commodity-wise trade potential information. If the RCA is more than 1 then the country has advantages in those goods, and if the RCA is less than 1 it means the country has disadvantage in that goods. Mathematically, $RCA = (x_{ij}/x_{it})/(x_{wj}/x_{wt})$, where x_{ij} is the export of *j* commodity in *i* country and, x_{it} is the total export of *i* country to world whereas x_{wj} is world export of *j* commodity and, x_{wt} is the total world export

Source: Calculated from WITS database, *Handbook of Statistics on Indian Economy*, RBI and (Annual Survey of Industries, various issues.)

trade orientation and revealed comparative advantage (RCA). It can be observed that during the 1990s, the RCA is found to be favourable for those industries for which the decrease in tariff is greater than 50 per cent. These industries are food, textile, metal and leather products. However, the decrease in tariff of these products is not found to be associated with import penetration and export orientation. In the case of non-metallic minerals, both import penetration and export orientation are found to be high, and RCA is found to be highly favourable for this product. For petroleum products, export orientation is associated with tariff decline.

During the 2000s, those products for which the decrease in tariff rate is greater than 20 per cent have witnessed a higher average value of RCA. Particularly, for petroleum products, tariff rate is highly associated with export orientation, RCA and gross value added. These products are metals, chemicals, non-metallic minerals and leather. Non-metallic minerals have maintained higher import penetration in 2000. However, it is not able to maintain higher value of export orientation. As compared to 1991, during the 2000s, the import penetration for all the products has increased except wood and fuel. Also the export orientation for non-metallic minerals and wood has decreased. Non-metallic minerals have a very high value of GVA followed by fuel and metals. Comparing the RCA advantage for the two periods, it is observed that apart from the previous products, it has found to have moved in favour of chemical and petroleum products.

5.4 Interrelationship between Trade Liberalization, Trade Orientation and Comparative Advantage

In order to confirm the relationship between the indicators of trade liberalization, trade orientation and comparative advantage, correlation coefficients are calculated as shown in Table 5.5. During the 1990s, correlation coefficient of tariff reduction is found to be highly positive and significant for import penetration (88 %) and export orientation (88 %). The correlation coefficient between import penetration and export orientation (95 %) is positive and significant at 1 per cent level. RCA has a positive and significant relationship with GVA (65 %) at 5 per cent level. During the 2000s, tariff reduction is found to be positively and significantly correlated with import penetration (93 %) but not with export orientation. It is also positively and significantly correlated with RCA (68 %) at 5 per cent level and GVA (88 %) at 1 per cent level. Capital–labour ratio has a positive and significant

Table 5.5 Interrelationship between liberalization, trade orientation and comparative advantage

Indicators	*Time-period*	*Tariff reduction*	*FDI*	*K/L*	*Import penetration*	*Export orientation*	*Technological intensity*	*RCA*	*GVA*
Tariff	1990s	1.00							
reduction	2000s	1.00							
FDI	1990s	0.05	1.00						
	2000s	-0.11	1.00						
K/L	1990s	0.15	0.55	1.00					
	2000s	-0.02	0.07	1.00					
Import	1990s	0.88**	-0.20	0.02	1.00				
penetration.	2000s	0.93**	-0.10	-0.12	1.00				
Export	1990s	0.88**	-0.20	-0.07	0.95**	1.00			
orientation.	2000s	-0.09	-0.07	0.83**	-0.27	1.00			
Technological	1990s	-0.26	-0.58	-0.28	0.08	-0.07	1.00		
intensity	2000s	0.06	-0.52	-0.06	-0.04	-0.01	1.00		
RCA	1990s	0.45	-0.47	-0.31	0.51	0.56	0.38	1.00	
	2000s	0.68*	-0.18	-0.19	0.75**	-0.34	0.27	1.00	
GVA	1990s	0.13	0.01	-0.27	-0.05	-0.02	0.15	0.65*	1.00
	2000s	0.88**	0.04	0.22	0.92**	-0.03	-0.09	0.62*	1.00

**Correlation is significant at the 0.01 level (two-tailed)
*Correlation is significant at the 0.05 level (two-tailed)

Source: Computed

relationship with export orientation (83 %). Import penetration has a positive and significant relationship with RCA (75 %) and GVA (92 %) at 1 per cent level. RCA is also positively related with GVA (62 %) at 5 per cent level of significance. The correlation of FDI is not at all found to be significant with any of the selected variable. This indicates that the inflow of FDI is not taking care of the trade expansion, comparative advantage, value addition and technological advancement in Indian manufacturing industries. The higher and negative correlation coefficient of FDI with technological intensity is not strong enough to become significant. Still, it is giving some implication of the investment in relatively lower technology.

5.5 Conclusion

Trade liberalization has brought significant changes in the structure of Indian manufacturing industries. Over the period of time, the industries have become more capital intensive and technology intensive (skill biased). However, the growth rate of value added per worker does not commensurate with that of capital–labour ratio and FDI. This indicates that the labour efficiency is not matching with imported capital and technology under liberalization. The industry-wise comparison of structural changes show that the growth rate of capital–labour ratio increased particularly in low-technology and medium low-technology industries. Growth of FDI has increased in those industries that facilitate the production and transportation of finished goods. These are electrical equipment, computer, electronic and optical products, chemical and chemical products, and transportation. Further tariff reduction is found to be highly correlated with import penetration, RCA and GVA. The high correlation of import penetration with RCA and GVA show that decreases in trade barriers have facilitated the manufacturing exports as well as manufacturing growth. The high correlation coefficient between capital–labour ratio and export orientation shows that manufacture of export goods are highly based upon capital-intensive technology.

It is concluded that trade liberalization has shifted the structure of Indian manufacturing industries towards capital-intensive technology as well as skill-based technology. However, the weaker response of value added per worker reflects inefficiencies in the production structure.

Notes

1. These licences determined the scale, technology and location of investment projects and any plan to expand, relocate or change the output or input mixes that needed prior permission from the government (Srinivasan 2001).
2. Also discussed in Grossman and Helpman (1991) and Rivera-Batiz and Romer (1991).
3. Feenstra and Hanson (1997) argue that rapid expansion in 'outsourcing' or 'global production sharing' over the past two decades can explain part of the observed increase in demand for skilled labour.
4. Several studies have observed a decline in labour intensity across the manufacturing industries during the last two decades (Das et al. 2009; Rani and Unni 2004).
5. During the 2000s, the Indian economy has achieved an average growth rate of greater than 6 per cent (higher than the growth rate of developed countries)

References

Annual Survey of Industries, Summary Results for Factory Sector, weblink: http://mospi.nic.in/

Annual Survey of Industries, various issues, Annual Survey of Industries, weblink: http://mospi.nic.in/

Das, Deb Kusum, and Gujajit Kalita. (2009): "Are Labour-Intensive Industries Generating Employment in India? Evidence from Firm Level Survey", *The Indian Journal of Labour Economics*, Vol. 52(3).

Das, K.D., D. Wadhwa, and G. Kalita (2009): "The Employment Potential of Labour Intensive Industries in India's Organized Manufacturing", *Working Paper no 236*, Indian Council of Research on International Economic Relations.

Directorate General of Commercial Intelligence and Statistics (DGCI&S), Ministry of Commerce and Industry, GOI, weblink: http://www.dgciskol.nic.in/foreign_trade_statistics.asp

Feenstra, Robert C., and Gordon H. Hanson. (1997): "Foreign Direct Investment and Relative Wages: Evidence from Mexico's Maquiladoras", *Journal of International Economics*, Vol. 42(3-4), May.

Grossman, Gene, and Elhanan Helpman. (1991): *Innovation and Growth in the Global Economy*, MIT Press, Cambridge.

Handbook of Statistics on Indian Economy, Reserve Bank of India, weblink: https://rbidocs.rbi.org.in/.

Hummels, David, Jun Ishii, and Kei-Mu Yi. (2001): "The Nature and Growth of Vertical Specialization in World Trade", *Journal of International Economics*, Vol. 54.

Lee, H.Y., L.A. Ricci, and R. Rigobon. (2004): "Once Again, Is Openness Good for the Growth?", *Journal of Development Economics*, Vol. 75.

Nathan, Dev, and Anne Posthuma. (2009): "Implications of Global Production for Indian Firms and Labour: An Introduction", *The Indian Journal of Labour Economics*, Vol. 42(4).

Paul, B.P., and A. Das. (2012): "Openness and Output Dynamics in South Asia", *Indian Economic Journal*, Vol. 59(4), January–March.

Rani, U., and J. Unni. (2004): "Unorganized and Organized Manufacturing in India: Potential for Employment Generating Growth", *Economic and Political Weekly*, Vol. 39(41).

Rivera-Batiz, Luis, and Paul Romer. (1991): "Economic Integration and Endogenous Growth", *Quarterly Journal of Economics*, Vol. 106(2).

Roy, Satyaki (2008): "Skill Premium: What Caused the 'Mismatch'?", *MPRA Paper No. 18010*, weblink: https://mpra.ub.uni-muenchen.de/18010/1/MPRA_paper_18010.pdf accessed on 20-11-2013.

Sadhukhan, Amit (n.d.): Trade, Technology, and Institution: How Do They Affect Wage Inequality in Indian Manufacturing, weblink: http://www.cdedse.org/ws2011/papers/amit%20sadhukhan.Pdf accessed on 24-12-2013.

Srinivasan, T.N. (2001): "Economic Reforms and Global Integration", *Working Paper No. 120*, Centre for Research and Economic Development and Policy Reform, Stanford University, November

Sunder, K.R. Shyam. (2012): "Counter Tendencies to Labour Flexibility Regime in India: Achieving Decent Work for Non-Regular Workers", *Indian Journal of Labour Economics*, Vol. 55(4).

Wood, Adrian. (1994): *North-South Trade, Employment and Inequality: Changing Fortunes in a Skill-Driven World*, Clarendon Press, Oxford.

Wood, Adrian. (1997): "Openness and Wage Inequality in Developing Countries: The Latin American Challenge to East Asian Conventional Wisdom", *World Bank Economic Review*, Vol. 11(1), 33–58.

World Integrated Trade Solution (WITS), weblink: www.wits.worldbank.org

CHAPTER 6

Trade Liberalization, Manufacturing Growth and Environmental Externalities

Abstract Chapter 4 shows that India has major trade and investment relationship with developed countries of the world. Chapter 5 show that the structure and pattern of Indian manufacturing industries has changed over the past two and half decades. Taking into account the differences in environmental norms between the developed and developing countries, there is a concern that whether trade-oriented manufacturing growth is generating any environmental externality in India. This chapter examines the trends of manufacturing growth and pollution concentration in India, finds the relationship between manufacturing output and pollution loads at industry level and estimates the impact of manufacturing growth on environmental externalities by decomposing the total trade effect into scale, composition and technique effects.

Keywords Manufacturing growth · Pollution loads · Estimations

Trade liberalization, nowadays, is considered to be a means to promote economic growth. It imparts both efficiency and dynamism to the growth process. A liberal trade policy by facilitating the inflows of capital, investment and technology enables the less developed countries to expand their scale of manufacturing activity. The present-day trade policy is highly focused on export orientation, i.e. production for exports. This motivated the producers of the developing countries to import intermediates, capital

H. Jain, *Trade Liberalisation, Economic Growth and Environmental Externalities*, DOI 10.1007/978-981-10-2887-8_6

and technologies from the world in order to increase their exports by expanding their scale of production. All the trade theories have considered that a country specializes in production of those commodities in which it has a comparative cost advantage. Since the implementation of environmental policies raises the cost of production of domestic industry and thus adversely influences the competitiveness of domestic producers in the world market, there is a high possibility that on behalf of trade liberalization, the countries with stricter environmental norms (particularly developed countries) may choose to relocate their production activities to countries with weaker environmental policies (particularly developing countries). This may result into 'pollution havens' in developing countries. Since market in developing countries is not able to capture this environmental loss, it is regarded as environmental externality. These externalities have higher social cost then benefits, thus it adversely affects the social well-being.

Chapter 4 shows that India has major trade relationships with developed countries of the world. Also, a maximum amount of FDI as well as technology is sourced from the developed countries. On account of this, as observed in Chapter 5, the structure and pattern of Indian manufacturing industries has changed over the past two and half decades. Two conflicting situation is observed: (i) the industries have become more capital intensive. According to Rastogi and Sawhney (2013), pollution-intensive industries are generally capital intensive. Also India's comparative advantage is higher in exports based on low technologies. Imports have also increased in low-technology industries. (ii) The FDI has decreased in low-technology industries and increased in moderate- and high-technology-based industries. Also, the foreign technology collaboration is higher in high-technology-based industries. It is a common phenomenon that with increase in income, a shift from low technology to moderate technology and finally to high technology occurs. High-technology-based industries have high intensity of research and development (R&D), which implies more efficiency and less pollution in the long run. The absorption of imported technologies requires some technological capability on the part of the hosting firm. Also imported plants and machinery may also require adaptation and modifications to suit the local conditions and raw materials and usage pattern.[1] This requires investment in R&D activities.[2] However, India lacks in terms of both skill and R&D expenditure. The World

Development Indicators show that India is spending only 0.8 per cent of its GDP on R&D, while in developed countries it ranges up to 35 per cent.

Taking into consideration the high growth of Indian economy during the past decade and structural shifts in the manufacturing industries in favour of capital-intensive technologies, the following question arises: (i) Has India achieved this growth by specializing in pollution-intensive (low-technology) industries? (ii) To what extent the trade-led high economic growth of India is able to shift the production activities to relatively clean technologies?[3] (iii) How do the growth associated with other developmental factors (education, skill, infrastructural facilities, etc.) contribute to clean environment?[4]

The present chapter is structured as follows: Section 6.1 examines the trends of manufacturing growth and pollution concentration in India. Section 6.2 finds the relationship between manufacturing output and pollution loads at industry level. Section 6.3 estimates the impact of manufacturing growth on environmental externalities in terms of scale effect, composition effect and technique effect. Section 6.4 concludes the chapter.

6.1 Manufacturing Growth and Pollution Concentration in India

The expansion of manufacturing activities generates externalities for the environment depending upon the level of technologies employed. If the scale of output expands in the industries based on low-level technology, the quality of environment may deteriorate and vice versa. Figure 6.1 shows the trends in manufacturing output and pollution loads during the selected periods. Pollution loads are calculated for Indian manufacturing industries with the help of IPPS coefficients developed by World Bank. Since the expansion of manufacturing activity alters the quality of environment, pollution loads are obtained with respect to manufacturing output. The figure reveals that both the manufacturing output and pollution loads have continuously increased. A closer look at the height of the columns in the figures shows that the period during which the increase in output was high (2004–05/2009–10), the increase in industrial pollution loads was also high.

Table 6.1 shows that on an average, during 2004/05 to 2009/10, manufacturing output has increased by around 12 per cent while pollution load has increased by 24 per cent. During this period, investment has

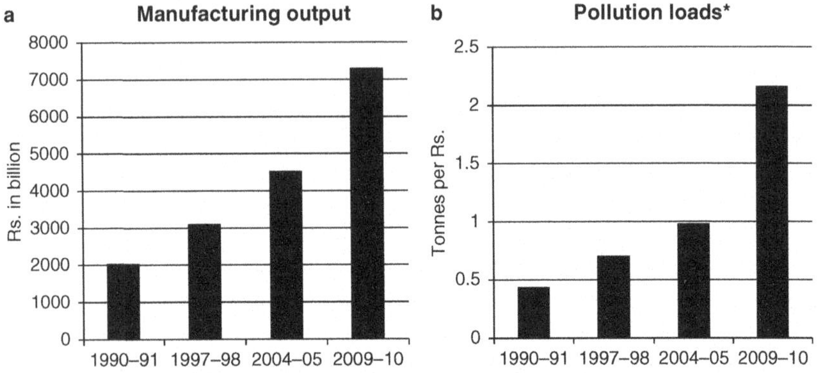

Fig. 6.1 (a) Manufacturing output. *Source*: Author's calculation from Annual Survey of Industries. (b) Pollution loads. *Calculated for manufacturing industries. *Source*: Author's calculation based on IPPS coefficients

Table 6.1 Per annum change in manufacturing output and pollution concentration (%)

Time period	*Manufacturing output*	*Pollution load*
1990/91–1997/98	6.65	7.74
1997/98–2004/05	5.69	4.89
2004/05–2009/10	12.23	23.99

Source: Based on Fig. 6.1

remarkably increased in some specific industries, like petroleum product, chemicals, textiles, non-metallic minerals, metals and electrical equipment. Among them, petroleum product, chemicals, textiles, metals and electronic goods are dominating in India's exports.

6.1.1 Decomposition of Industrial Pollution Loads

On decomposing the industrial pollution load into air, water and toxic pollution (as shown in Table 6.2), it is observed that air pollution accounts for the maximum amount of industrial pollution. A further decomposition of the pollutants show that among the various air pollutants, the concentration of SO_2 appears to be very high followed by NO_2 and CO. The high

Table 6.2 Summary statistics of industrial pollutants (in kg /Rs. output)

Pollutants	*Mean*		*Std. Deviation*		*Maximum*	
	1990–91	*2009–10*	*1990–91*	*2009–10*	*1990–91*	*2009–10*
			Air pollution			
SO_2	0.3756	1.1794	2.2174	6.4893	22.1166	63.6338
NO_2	0.1919	0.6549	1.0681	3.4888	10.2689	29.5456
CO	0.0862	0.2791	0.2912	0.9611	1.7436	6.7045
VOC	0.0012	0.0051	0.0030	0.0191	0.0250	0.1465
FP	0.0025	0.0073	0.0239	0.0687	0.2424	0.6973
TSP	0.0019	0.0057	0.0139	0.0401	0.1410	0.4056
			Water pollution			
BOD	0.0003	0.0007	0.0018	0.0039	0.0175	0.0359
TSS	0.0019	0.0055	0.0080	0.0250	0.0576	0.2215
			Toxic			
Air	0.0008	0.0028	0.0021	0.0097	0.0144	0.0846
Land	0.0009	0.0026	0.0026	0.0088	0.0139	0.0701
Water	0.0000	0.0001	0.0001	0.0006	0.0011	0.0062

Source: Author's calculation for World Bank Industrial Pollution Projection System

magnitude of standard deviation and a greater difference between the maximum value and mean value implies that emission of pollutants is highly uneven among the manufacturing industries.

6.1.2 *Industries under Various Types of Pollutants*

Further, the industries are distributed according to the various types of pollutants. Table 6.3 shows that during 1990–91, number of industries above the average pollution level of SO_2 was only 34 out of 103. This number strikingly declined to 12 in 1997–98 and remained as such till 2009–10. Matching these figures with the previous Table 6.2 reflects that only 12 per cent of the total industries are responsible for the high level of industrial pollution in the country. The loads for the other pollutants have also shown a decline during the selected years. This implies that from 2004–05 to 2009–10, the number of industries above the average pollution level for the major pollutants (SO_2 and NO_2) has remained almost the same. But their pollution loads have increased.

Table 6.3 Distribution of industries according to pollution loads

Pollutants	*Above average*				*Total no. of industries*
	1990–91	*1997–98*	*2004–05*	*2009–10*	
		Air pollution			
SO_2	34	12	11	12	103
NO_2	9	8	9	9	103
CO	11	10	10	12	103
VOC	26	18	8	12	103
FA	2	2	2	2	103
TSP	9	10	5	8	103
		Water pollution			
BOD	7	6	8	7	103
TSS	10	11	9	9	103
		Toxic pollution			
Air	24	14	9	15	103
Land	13	12	14	14	103
Water	20	7	10	12	103

Source: Author's calculation for World Bank Industrial Pollution Projection System

6.2 Relation between Manufacturing Output and Pollution Loads at Industry Level

Further, to identify whether the highly producing industries are responsible for the high level of pollution, the industries are ranked in descending order according to their output and pollution loads. Tables 6.4 and 6.5 show the ranks of highly producing industries and highly polluting industries in descending order (disaggregated at four digit of NIC 2008). In order to determine the shift in the composition of highly producing industries, comparison is done for 4 years of the post-reform period. A bird's eye view of the table shows that high technology industries are gradually climbing the ladder of industrial output. During 1990–91, the top three position in terms of highest production was occupied by food product that is based on low technology. In 2009–10, this position is taken by moderately high-technology and high-technology industries, particularly motor vehicles and drugs and pharmaceuticals, while low-technology industries are gradually going

Table 6.4 Top 10 highly producing industries

Rank	*1990–91*	*1997–98*	*2004–05*	*2009–10*
1	Vegetable and animal oils and fats (LT)	Vegetable and animal oils and fats (LT)	Motor vehicles (MHT)	Motor vehicles (MHT)
2	Sugar (LT)	Drugs and pharmaceuticals (HT)	Vegetable and animal oils and fats (LT)	Drugs and pharmaceuticals (HT)
3	Grain mill (LT)	Grain mill (LT)	Basic precious and other non-ferrous metals (MLT)	Vegetable and animal oils and fats (LT)
4	Drugs and pharmaceuticals (HT)	Plastic and synthetic rubber in primary forms (MLT)	Drugs and pharmaceuticals (HT)	Grain mill (LT)
5	Cement, lime and plaster (MLT)	Sugar (LT)	Grain mill (LT)	Plastic and synthetic rubber in primary forms (MLT)
6	Fabricated metal products (MLT)	Basic precious and other non-ferrous metals (MLT)	Plastic and synthetic rubber in primary forms (MLT)	Basic precious and other non-ferrous metals (MLT)
7	Fertilizer and nitrogen compounds (MHT)	Cement, lime and plaster (MLT)	Transport equipment (MHT)	Cement, lime and plaster (MLT)
8	Pesticides and other agrochemical products (MHT)	Electrical equipment (MHT)	Electrical equipment (MHT)	Electrical equipment (MHT)
9	Basic precious and other non-ferrous metals (MLT)	Fertilizer and nitrogen compounds (MHT)	Paper and paper products (LT)	Sugar (LT)
10	Pulp, paper and paper board (LT)	Dairy products (LT)	Sugar (LT)	Fertilizer and nitrogen compounds (MHT)

Note: Technology groups are given in Annexure A 5.1

LT: low technology, MLT: medium-low technology, MHT: medium-high technology, HT: high technology.

Source: Author's calculation based on Annual Survey of Industries

Table 6.5 Top 10 highly polluting industries

Rank	*1990–91*	*1997–98*	*2004–05*	*2009–10*
1	Cement, lime and plaster (MLT)	Cement, lime and plaster (MLT)	Basic precious and other non-ferrous metals (MLT)	Cement, lime and plaster (MLT)
2	Vegetable and animal oils and fats (LT)	Vegetable and animal oils and fats (LT)	Cement, lime and plaster (MLT)	Basic precious and other non-ferrous metals (MLT)
3	Basic precious and other non-ferrous metals (MLT)	Basic precious and other non-ferrous metals (MLT)	Vegetable and animal oils and fats (LT)	Vegetable and animal oils and fats (LT)
4	Coke and refined petroleum (MLT)	Plastic and synthetic rubber in primary form (MLT)	Plastic and synthetic rubber in primary form (MLT)	Casting iron and steel (MLT)
5	Plastic and synthetic rubber in primary form (MLT)	Coke and refined petroleum (MLT)	Casting iron and steel (MLT)	Other chemical products* (MHT)
6	Casting iron and steel (MLT)	Casting iron and steel (MLT)	Coke and refined petroleum (MLT)	Plastic and synthetic rubber in primary form (MLT)
7	Casting non-ferrous metals (MLT)	Casting non-ferrous metals (MLT)	Other chemical products* (MHT)	Coke and refined petroleum (MLT)
8	Other chemical products* (MHT)	Other chemical products* (MHT)	Fertilizer and nitrogen compounds (MHT)	Drugs and pharmaceuticals (HT)
9	Drugs and pharmaceuticals (HT)	Drugs and pharmaceuticals (HT)	Drugs and pharmaceuticals (HT)	Fertilizer and nitrogen compounds (MHT)
10	Fertilizer and nitrogen compounds (MHT)	Fertilizer and nitrogen compounds (MHT)	Casting non-ferrous metals (MLT)	Rubber tyres and (MLT) tubes

*Includes pesticides and other agrochemical products, paints, varnishes and similar coating, printing ink and mastics, soap and detergents, cleaning and polishing preparations, perfumes and toilet preparations

Note: Technology groups are given in Annexure A 5.1

LT: low technology, MLT: medium-low technology, MHT: medium-high technology, HT: high technology

Source: Author's calculation based on Annual Survey of Industries, and IPPS coefficients

Table 6.6 Rank correlation between pollution loads and manufacturing output

Variables	*Pollution loads*			
	1990–91	*1997–98*	*2004–05*	*2009–10*
Manufacturing output	0.796	0.720	0.629	0.446

Source: Author's calculation

down. This implies that high technology industries are gradually gaining importance for increasing the manufacturing output.

Table 6.5 shows the top 10 highly polluting industries in India for the selected years. It is observed that the highly polluting industries contain a mix of all type of technologies. Low- and moderately low-technology industries are leading in terms of highly polluting categories. On matching the ranks of highly polluting industries (Table 6.5) with that of highly producing industries (Table 6.4), it can be seen that more than half of the industries in the top 10 ranks are similar in both the tables. Such industries are drugs and pharmaceuticals, vegetable and animal oils and fats, plastic and synthetic rubber in primary forms, basic precious and other non-ferrous metals, cement, lime and plaster, and fertilizer and nitrogen compounds.

Further to clarify the relationship between manufacturing output and pollution loads, rank correlation coefficients are obtained for all the industries as given in Annual Survey Industries at 4-digit classification as shown in Table 6.6. It is revealed that the rank correlation coefficient between the manufacturing output and pollution loads over the years is decreasing. It was 80 per cent in 1990–91 which decreased to 45 per cent in 2009–10. This implies that apart from the scale of manufacturing activity, there is a need to focus on the other factors that affects pollution concentration. They may be change in technology or some other factors that facilitates the process of production, for example, increase in qualified personnel, acquisition of skill, development of facilities (like roads, information and communication technology and electrification) and so on.

6.3 Estimation of the Impact of Manufacturing Growth on Environmental Externalities

Considering that the impact of manufacturing growth on environmental externalities changes with time, the estimates are obtained separately for scale, composition and technique effects by ordinary least square (OLS) method. Scale effect is related with the increase in manufacturing activity, composition effect reflects specialization achieved by the nation due to increased trade-related activities, and the technique effect shows the impact of economic growth. All these effects are shown in Table 6.7. Regression results are obtained for the SO_2 and NO_2 as these pollutants account for the highest share in total pollution load of manufacturing industries. Among the core variables representing the scale, composition and technique effects, the scale of manufacturing activity (as measured by manufacturing output/km^2 area) is found to be positively and significantly related with the industrial pollution load in all the three models of SO_2 and NO_2. The elasticity of concentration of SO_2 with respect to an increase in scale of manufacturing activity (as shown in the bottom of the table) is found to vary from 0.4 to 1.2. For NO_2, it is found to vary between 0.3 and 1.2. From the log likelihood ratio, it appears that there is gain in moving to the slightly more general model C from models A and B. In the composition effect, the impact of capital–labour ratio on industrial pollution load is positive and significant in model A for both the pollutants. It is found to be negative and significant in model C indicating that with constant scale and technology, an increase in capital–labour ratio decreases the pollution loads. The composition elasticity shows that a 1 per cent increase in capital–labour ratio decreases SO_2 concentration by 0.25 per cent and NO_2 concentration by 1.08 per cent. The estimates for technique effect show that the impact of per capita income on pollution load is not at all significant. Surprisingly, the technique elasticity is showing an increase in pollution load with 1 per cent increase in per capita income. The technique elasticity appears to be quite large in model C for both NO_2 and SO_2.

Further effect of trade liberalization on pollution load in India shows surprising results. The further rise in scale of manufacturing activity is showing a negative and significant impact on pollution loads. Similar effect is shown by the accumulation of capital via increased openness. The impact of income gain is found to be negative but insignificant. If we take into account the income gain brought about by capital accumulation, the effect on pollution load is positive and significant. The impact of the time dummy is found to be negative and insignificant. It is to be noted here that when the same models were tried with ignoring the time dummy, the results were irrelevant. The inclusion of time dummy in the model increased the relevance of the selected variables. This indicates that trade expansion with trade liberalization is sure to decrease industrial pollution loads. However, the estimates for India are totally different from other studies. For the

Table 6.7 Estimation results

Explanatory Variables	*Dependent variables*					
	SO_2			*NO_2*		
	Model A	*Model B*	*Model C*	*Model A*	*Model B*	*Model C*
Constant	−0.0509	−2.8100	−6.3600	−0.0609	1.2400	−0.1340
			Scale effect			
MNA	2.4300**	1.5000**	4.1700**	0.7550**	0.4720**	1.5100**
MNA^2			−1.2000**			−0.4660**
			Composition effect			
KLR	0.1060**	−0.0044	−0.0220*	0.0679	−0.0337	−0.0405*
KLR^2		−0.0042**	−0.0041**		−0.0009**	−0.0009**
			Technique effect			
PCI	0.0000	0.0004	0.0008	0.0000	−0.0001	0.0000
PCI^2		0.0000	0.0000		0.0000	0.0000
			Combined effect of technique and composition			
PCIKLR		0.0000**	0.0000**		0.0000**	0.0000**
			Time-specific effect			
TD	−0.17	−0.90	−1.75	−0.08	0.24	−0.09
Observations	410	410	410	410	410	410
Cross-sections	103	103	103	103	103	103
R-squared	0.62	0.67	0.68	0.54	0.50	0.53

(*continued*)

Table 6.7 (continued)

Explanatory Variables	*Dependent variables*					
	SO_2			NO_2		
	Model A	*Model B*	*Model C*	*Model A*	*Model B*	*Model C*
Log likelihood	-9590.77	-9584.29	-9568.04	-9250.96	-9250.01	-9235.36
Scale elasticity	0.79	0.45	1.25	0.35	0.34	1.09
Composition elasticity	1.18	-4.87	-0.25	1.81	-9	-1.08
Technique elasticity	-0.03	1.82	38.38	0.05	3.84	14.89

Note: (1) ** and * represents significance at 1 % and 5 % levels, respectively
(2) Elasticities are calculated by Delta method

Source: Author's calculation

developed countries, per capita income dominates in reducing the pollution concentrations as higher income enables people to demand for cleaner technologies. But for India, per capita income is not found to be significant. Rather the scale and composition effects are found to be dominating the income effect. The inverted U-shape relationship of pollution loads with respect to manufacturing activity and continuous negative relationship of capital–labour ratio indicates inefficiencies in the scale of production.

6.4 Conclusion

India is a special case with high population concentration, high income inequality and poor skill. It has comparative advantage in labour-intensive technologies which are less pollution intensive. From the estimated results, it appears that an increase in industrial pollution is not due to inflow of capital-intensive technologies via trade liberalization. Rather it is due to inefficiencies in the production structure. A poor level of skill and infrastructural constraints are some of the factors that restrict the optimal utilization of capital which finally results into release of pollutants.

The study concludes that the pollution haven hypothesis is not significant for India. However the positive and significant impact of income gain combined with capital accumulation directs us to protect the economy from increasing pollution loads. Enriching the human beings with skill and knowledge along with environmental awareness will on the one hand, give an efficient scale of production with optimal utilization of capital, and on the other, will decrease the emissions.

Notes

1. See Cohen and Levinthal (1989) and Bell and Pavitt (1997).
2. See Mani (1995) and Basant (1997).
3. Economic growth enables the country to spare resources for research and development.
4. Free trade is good for the environment (Antweiler et al. 2001).

References

Annual Survey of Industries, weblink: http://mospi.nic.in/

Antweiler, W., B.R. Copeland, and M.S. Taylor. (2001): "Is Free Trade Good for the Environment?", *American Economic Review*, Vol. 91(4).

Basant, Rakesh. (1997): "Technology Strategies of Large Enterprises in Indian Industry: Some Explorations", *World Development*, Vol. 25.

Bell, Martin, and Keith Pavitt. (1997): "Technological Accumulation and Industrial Growth: Contrasts between Developed and Developing Countries", in Danele Archibugi and Jonathan Michie (ed.): *Technology, Globalisation and Economic Performance*, Cambridge University Press, Cambridge.

Cohen, Wesley M., and Daniel A. Levinthal. (1989): "Innovation and Learning: The Two Faces of R&D", *The Economic Journal*, Vol. 99.

Mani, Sunil. (1995): "Technology Import and Skill Development in a Microelectronics Based Industry: The case of India's Electronic Switching Systems", in Amiya Kumar Bagchi (ed.): *New Technology and the Worker's Response*, Sage Publication, New Delhi.

Rastogi, Rashmi, and Aparna Sawhney. (2013): "What Attracts FDI in Indian Manufacturing Industries?", *Discussion Paper 13-02*, Centre for International Trade and Development, School of International Studies, Jawaharlal Nehru University, India.

CHAPTER 7

Environmental Externality and Well-Being: A Micro-Level Approach with a Focus on Gujarat

Abstract This chapter deals with the micro-level approach to find the impact of industrial pollution on the well-being of the local people living at a radius of 10 km from industrial location. The chapter presents the results of the survey conducted for two industries of Gujarat. After giving an overview of the selected area and sample characteristics, the chapter focuses on the household's awareness about industrial emissions, respondent's opinion about the impact of industrial pollution on agricultural productivity, livestock and human health and, finally, the estimation results. Since the impact of pollution on society varies according to socio-economic and industry-based factors, the variables related to demographic characteristics, occupational structure, educational and housing status and agricultural status of the household as well as pollution-related variables were taken into consideration.

Keywords Gujarat · Micro-level approach · Estimations

Manufacturing growth is essential for accelerating the economic growth of a nation. But expanding the manufacturing activity in an inefficient manner (with low technology base, inefficient manpower, improper infrastructural facilities, etc.) generates environmental externalities. These environmental externalities create disutility for the society; more influenced are the people living close to the industrial set-ups.

H. Jain, *Trade Liberalisation, Economic Growth and Environmental Externalities*, DOI 10.1007/978-981-10-2887-8_7

The past few years have experienced establishment of industries in the rural areas. This includes new industrial establishments, relocation of industries from urban areas to rural areas as well as shifting of industries from abroad under the process of trade liberalization. Rural economy has a predominance of agricultural activity that highly depends upon the quality of natural resources (particularly soil, air and water). On the contrary, the manufacturing industries consider these resources for dumping their pollution. Though, before initiating a project or for expansion or modernization of existing industry, the industrialists have to seek environmental clearance from the Ministry of Environment and Forest, New Delhi. Also, for discharging the treated effluents, clearance is mandatory from the concerned State Pollution Control Board. The industries are also required to install effluent treatment plant.

Since keeping the emissions under the permissible limits imposes cost on the producers, protection of environment appears to be luxurious for them. Instead, they find it cheaper to pollute than to control the waste product. In the age of competition, the producers focus on increasing the productivity than to adopting the pollution control measures. Over the period of time, due to lack of maintenance, the installed effluent treatment plants stops functioning. The remoteness of the industries limits the visit of the monitoring agencies. Besides the pollution standards are formulated on the basis of new technologies, for which the outdated technologies face difficulty in complying with it. Also due to lack of awareness, political lobbying, etc., the villagers are not empowered to raise their voices. All these make the industrialists relaxed towards maintaining the environmental quality.

Decrease in environmental quality has both short- and long-term consequences. In the short run, the pollution does not affect the industrial productivity, but it has severe consequences for the agricultural productivity. The release of smoke spoils the standing crops. The discharge of waste water depletes the underground water. The result is decrease in agricultural income, loss of employment, increase in poverty and increase in prices of food products. In the long run, the depleted environment affects not only the agricultural and the industrial sector, but also the human health. The long-term exposure to effluents decreases the soil fertility. This makes the agricultural practice non-remunerative and non-viable. The industries that are dependent on agricultural inputs face severe supply constraint. Social disutility arises in terms of decrease in human health and quality of life. The decline in health makes the human being economically unproductive. This undermines the future productivity. The deprivation in health of local population is not a major problem for the industries as they are now following mechanization with capital inflows. Also majority of the industrial workers commute from other places.

On the one hand, India is facing a problem of rural poverty, unemployment and food insecurity and, on the other hand, the agricultural land surrounding the industries is losing its productivity. In a country like India, having a high growth rate of population, agriculture is the mainstay for providing livelihood to millions of people. Since the concentration of pollution decreases with increase in distance from the industrial set-up, it can be said that the population in the villages in the immediate surroundings of the industry is more vulnerable to the effects of industrial pollution.

The study adopts a micro-level approach to find the impact of industrial pollution on the well-being of the local people. Within India, Gujarat state industrial policy is highly open for foreign direct investment, capital inflows and industrial relocations from abroad. After the economic reforms, Gujarat has attracted maximum FDI and has achieved second position in industrialization after Maharashtra. Therefore, Gujarat serves as a good laboratory for determining the impact of trade-induced environmental externalities on social well-being.

The study is conducted on two industries of Gujarat, namely petroleum refinery in Jamnagar district (Region 1) and fertilizer and chemicals industry in Vadodara district (Region 2). These industries are selected on the basis of their output and pollution loads. The chapter produces the results of the field survey conducted in the villages surrounding these industries at a distance of 10 km. Apart from the nature of the industry, the villages are different in terms of their approach to the city, development of amenities, education and employment opportunities and facilities provided by the industries. These characteristics have an importance in determining the level of well-being.

The chapter proceeds as follows: Section 7.1 gives an overview of the industrial and agricultural status of Gujarat. Section 7.2 describes the sample characteristics. Section 7.3 shows the household's awareness about industrial emission. Section 7.4 presents respondent's opinion about the impact of industrial pollution on agricultural productivity, livestock and human health. Section 7.5 explains the results of ordinary logit model. Section 7.6 concludes the chapter.

7.1 Status of Gujarat in India

7.1.1 Industrial Status in Terms of Output and Pollution Loads

There has been a rapid growth of industries in Gujarat during the past two decades. Table 7.1 shows the top 10 industries of Gujarat in terms of output for the years 1997–98 and 2009–10. Refined petroleum product is at the top position in 2009–10, followed by basic chemicals and fertilizers, basic iron and steel, textiles and other chemical products. On comparing the industrial output of top 10 industries in 2009–10 with that of 1997–98, it seems like industries are competing with one another to achieve the top position bypassing its side effects. The second part of the table shows the pollution load. Among the top 10 industries in terms of output, basic iron and steel, refined petroleum, basic precious and other non-ferrous metals, other chemical products and basic chemical and fertilizers are among the top five industries in terms of pollution loads. This gives an indication that after opening up of the economy, the tendency of industrial growth is significantly tilted towards the polluting industries.

7.1.2 Agricultural Status

During the decade 2001–2011, agricultural cultivators has decreased by 6.14 per cent which is much high as compared to that of India (Table 7.2). But in terms of agricultural labourers, the situation is very disappointing at both the state and the country levels. The agricultural labourer in Gujarat as well as in India during the decade has increased by more than 30 per cent. As a result, the total agricultural workforce has increased by nearly 12 per cent in Gujarat as well as in India. This indicates that the growth pattern is resulting into marginalization of the agricultural workforce. There has been some increase in the agricultural land area in Gujarat (2.48 %), though it is much less than the increase in agricultural workforce. The resulting increase in the pressure on land and decrease in labour productivity reflects the poor farm income and food insecurity. During this 10-year period, the agricultural output has increased by around 17 per cent in Gujarat, which is much less than the national average of 72 per cent. The comparison of the agricultural land area and agricultural output indicates the practicing of intensive cultivation. The share of

Table 7.1 Top 10 industries in terms of output and pollution loads

Sr. No.	*Industrial output*		*Pollution load*	
	1997–98	*2009–10*	*1997–98*	*2009–10*
1	Basic chemicals and fertilizers	Refined petroleum products	Basic iron and steel	Basic iron and steel
2	Textiles	Basic chemicals and fertilizers	Other chemical products	Refined petroleum products
3	Basic iron and steel	Basic iron and steel	Refined petroleum products	Basic precious and other non-ferrous metal
4	Refined petroleum products	Textiles	Basic chemicals and fertilizers	Other chemical products
5	Wearing apparel	Other chemical products	Textiles	Basic chemicals and fertilizers
6	Other chemical products	Transport equipment	Basic precious and other non-ferrous metal	Jewellery and related articles
7	Food products	Wearing apparel	Man-made fibres	Non-metallic mineral products
8	General purpose machinery	Non-metallic mineral products	Non-metallic mineral products	Textiles
9	Man-made fibres	Basic precious and other non-ferrous metal	Other fabricated metal products; metal working service activities	Other textiles
10	Paper and paper products	Optical instruments and equipment	General-purpose machinery	General purpose machinery

Source: Author's calculations based on Annual Survey of Industries, and IPPS coefficients developed by World Bank.

agriculture to Net State Domestic Product of Gujarat has decreased by 6 per cent and for India, it has decreased by around 10 per cent. This implies that non-agriculture sector is playing an important role in the growth of states as well as of the country.

Table 7.2 Agricultural status of Gujarat in India

Indicators	*Gujarat*			*India*		
	2001	*2011*	*Change (in %)*	*2001*	*2011*	*Change (in %)*
Agricultural cultivation	5,802,681	5446,500	-6.14	127,312,851	118,692,640	-0.07
Agricultural labour	5,161,658	6,839,415	+32.50	106,775,330	144,329,833	+35.17
Total agricultural workforce	10,964,339	12,285,915	+12.05	234,088,181	263,022,473	+12.36
Agricultural land area (in thousand hec)	12,354	12,661	+2.48	1,83,506	182,032	-0.80
Agricultural output (Rs. in crore)	32,809.29	38,481	17.3	708,903.5	1,220,278	72.1
Share of agriculture in domestic product (in %)	18.28	12.70	-5.58	24.93	14.51	-10.42

Source: Census of India, 2001 and 2011

7.2 Sample Characteristics

As shown in Table 7.3, majority of the sampled households are from general category (76%). Almost 95 per cent have their own house. The status of the house, education and awareness generating assets shows that the standard of living is not good in the selected villages. It is relatively poor in Region 1 as compared to Region 2. Region 1 comprises the remote villages and Region 2 is near the town Vadodara. The dependency level is high as nearly 50 per cent of the population is economically inactive. About 39 per cent population from the selected households are engaged in agricultural and 12 per cent in non-agricultural activity, while around 1 per cent engage in both the activities. This indicates fewer opportunities in the non-farm sector in selected villages. Besides, more than 50 per cent of the farmers have marginal land, and 30 per cent have small-size agricultural land. Only 18 per cent have large-size land.

Mechanization of agricultural activity, on the one hand, shows the status of the farmer and, on the other hand, eases the process of cultivation. Only

Table 7.3 Sample characteristics

S.No.		*Characteristics*	*Region 1*	*Region 2*	*Total*
1.	Total no. of households		50	50	100
2.	Caste	General	42 (84.0)	34 (68.0)	76 (76.0)
		OBC	3 (6.0)	13 (26.0)	16 (16.0)
		SC	3 (6.0)	2 (4.0)	5 (5.0)
		Muslim	2 (4.0)	1 (2.0)	3 (3.0)
3.	Females in the households (in %)		119 (44.40)	170 (54.14)	289 (49.27)
4.	Ownership of house	Own	47 (94.0)	48 (96.0)	95 (95.0)
		Rented	3 (6.0)	2 (4.0)	5 (5.0)
5.	Family size	2 to 4	20 (40.0)	11 (22.0)	31 (31.0)
		4 to 6	20 (40.0)	23 (46.0)	43 (43.0)
		6 to 8	6 (12.0)	5 (10.0)	11 (11.0)
		>8	4 (8.0)	11 (22.0)	15 (15.0)
6.	Type of house	Kuccha	4 (8.0)	3 (6.00	7 (7.0)
		Pukka	3 (6.0)	2 (4.0)	5 (5.0)
		Semi-pukka	43 (86.0)	45 (90.0)	88 (88.0)
7.	Education level of family	Up to 5th std	55 (20.52)	70 (22.29)	125 (21.41)
		5th to 10th std	109 (40.67)	133 (42.36)	242 (42.52)
		Above 10th std	29 (10.82)	8 (18.47)	87 (14.65)

(continued)

Table 7.3 (continued)

S.No.		*Characteristics*	*Region 1*	*Region 2*	*Total*
8.	Awareness-generating assets	Television	37 (74.0)	44 (88.0)	81 (81.0)
		Dish connection	29 (58.0)	36 (72.0)	65 (65.0)
		Mobile/ landline	45 (90.0)	47 (84.0)	92 (92.0)
		Computer	3 (6.0)	7 (14.0)	10 (10.0)
		Internet	3 (6.0)	3 (6.0)	6 (6.0)
		Two wheeler	19 (38.0)	31 (62.0)	50 (50.0)
		Four wheeler	6 (12.0)	6 (12.0)	12 (12.0)
9.	Occupational structure of the family	Agriculture	104 (38.80)	109 (34.71)	213 (36.76)
		Non-agriculture	33 (12.31)	39 (12.42)	72 (12.37)
		Both agriculture and non-agriculture	4 (1.49)	3 (0.09)	7 (0.79)
		Non-working	128 (47.76)	163 (51.91)	291 (49.83)
10.	Farmer category	Marginal	17 (34.0)	35 (70.0)	52 (52.0)
		Small	17 (34.0)	13 (26.0)	30 (30.0)
		Large	16 (32.0)	2 (4.0)	18 (18.0)
11.	Agricultural assets owned	Tractor	12 (24.0)	15 (30.0)	27 (27.0)
		Pumpset	19 (38.0)	10 (20.0)	29 (29.0)
		Plough		9 (18.0)	
		Land leveller		6 (12.0)	
		Pesticide pump	28 (56.0)	21 (42.0)	49 (49.0)
		Thresher	4 (8.0)	4 (8.0)	8 (8.0)
		Other	0(0.0)	10 (20.0)	10 (10.0)
12.	Livestock owned	Cow	21 (42.0)	8 (16.0)	29 (29.0)
		Buffalo	22 (44.0)	25 (50.0)	47 (47.0)
		Goat	12 (24.0)	0 (0.0)	12 (12.0)
		Ox	16 (32.0)	0 (0.0)	16 (16.0)
13.	Income from agriculture (in Rs.)	<20,000	1 (2.0)	15 (30.0)	16 (16.0)
		20,000–30,000	8 (16.0)	6 (12.0)	14 (14.0)
		30,000–40,000	4 (8.0)	2 (4.0)	6 (6.0)
		40,000–50,000	7 (14.0)	2 (4.0)	9 (9.0)
		50,000–60,000	6 (12.0)	3 (6.0)	9 (9.0)
		>60,000	24 (48.0)	22 (44.0)	46 (46.0)
14.	Annual Family income (Rs. in lakh)	0 to 0.5 lakh	11 (22.0)	11 (22.0)	22 (22.0)
		0.5 to 1 lakh	16 (32.0)	10 (20.0)	26 (26.0)
		1 to 3 lakh	16 (32.0)	22 (44.0)	38 (38.0)
		3 to 5 lakh	4 (8.0)	5 (10.0)	9 (9.0)
		5 to 7 lakh	1 (2.0)	1 (2.0)	2 92.0)
		>7 lakh	2 (4.0)	1 (2.0)	3 (3.0)

Source: Field-based information

27 per cent of the study households in Region 1 were found to have tractor, 29 per cent have pumpset and 49 per cent have pesticide pump. Animal power in agricultural farm is used by 16 per cent of the respondents. Majority of the livestock owned is cow and buffalo (mainly for milk production). Livestock rearing is prominent is Region 1 as compared to Region 2. About 70 per cent in Region 1 and 58 per cent in Region 2 have reported that they arrange fodder from their own agricultural field only. More than half of the population have annual income less than Rs. 60,000 from agriculture out of which about 30 per cent have their agricultural income up to Rs. 30,000. This indicates poverty in agriculture.

More than 85 per cent of the study households have their family income up to Rs. 3 lakh per annum. This indicates the existence of rural poverty.

7.3 Household's Awareness about Industrial Emission

Further the information was obtained for the households awareness about industrial emission and its implication for agricultural productivity (Figs 7.1 and 7.2). More than 90 per cent of the respondents in Region 1 have reported for all the three types of pollution while their percentage varies between 78 and 98 per cent in Region 2. One can feel the toxic smell of these

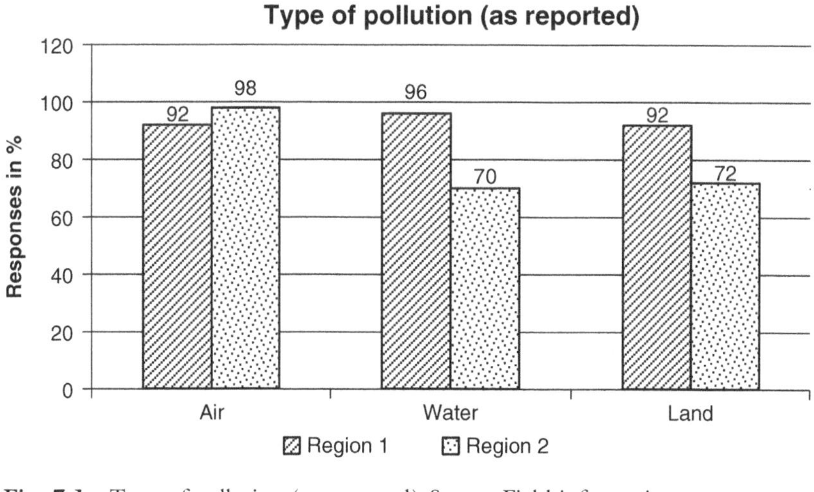

Fig. 7.1 Type of pollution (as reported) *Source*: Field information

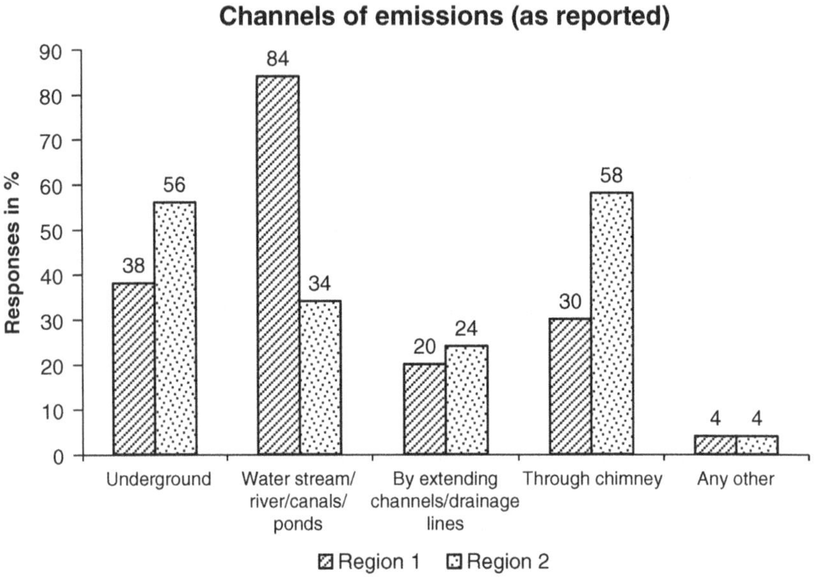

Fig. 7.2 Channels of emissions (as reported) *Source*: Field information

emissions in a radius of around 10 km from the industry followed by watery eyes, throat irritation and nausea (sometimes). Eighty-three per cent have reported for polluted water. Due to industrial emission, the underground as well as the river/canal water has become acidic in all the villages. The underground water in Vadinar is found to have an oily layer. In some villages of Region 1, the river water (Mithoi River) has become blackish in colour. In all, 82 per cent have reported for land pollution as land has become saline and unfertile near the industries. In Bajwa village[1] of Region 1, due to depletion of water, all the farmers have left agriculture and livestock rearing and many of them have become footloose.

As reported by the sampled household, these emissions mainly take place through injecting of untreated water into the ground (47 %), releasing the untreated water into the water streams/ river/canals/ponds by extending channels/drainage line that finally goes into the sea. One can see the dirty sea shores (*dariya*) due to industrial wastes. Smoke is released especially when the weather is cloudy or at night. These responses depend not only upon the geographical and hydrological factors that determines the direction of air and underground water flows, but also upon the industrial influence in terms of job opportunities; developmental works like schools, hospitals and water supply; and politics (especially elections of the village sarpanch). Therefore, in some cases, the responses obtained were biased in favour of industries. It was cross-checked through more discussions. The impact of pollution decreases with distance.

7.4 Respondent's Opinion about the Impact of Industrial Pollution

7.4.1 On Agricultural Productivity

Regarding the impact of industrial pollution on agriculture, majority of respondents have reported for the decline in the quality of crops (Table 7.4). Due to decrease in the size of grain, they get lesser price in the market. Apart from this, due to the increase in use of human power in agriculture, the cost of production has increased. Burning of leaves, less flowering and falling of flowers is the common problem. Land productivity has decreased. Availability of fodder has also decreased.

Table 7.5 shows the crop-wise changes in agricultural productivity. During the last 10 years, the productivity of wheat has decreased by 38 per cent while that of bajra and jowar has almost become half. The households have reported that pollution has more impact on wheat, bajra and jowar and also on mango trees. The production of mangoes has almost become zero as the flowers are not able to stay for long.

Table 7.4 Impact of industrial emissions (as reported)

S.No.	*Impact*	*Region 1*	*Region 2*
1.	Decrease in production	48 (96.0)	49 (98.0)
2.	Decline in crop quality	47 (94.0)	49 (98.0)
3.	Decrease in availability of fodder	40 (80.0)	32 (64.0)
4.	Less flower/falling of flowers	33 (66.0)	45 (90.0)
5.	Burning of leaves	40 (80.0)	42 (84.0)
6.	Intensive cultivation	45 (90.0)	47 (94.0)
7.	Increase in use of human power	44 (88.0)	41 (82.0)
8.	Cost of production has increased	47 (94.0)	48 (96.0)

Figures in parentheses show percentage of respondents.
Source: Field survey

Table 7.5 Average agricultural productivity during the last 10 years (as reported) (in quintal per acre)

Crop	*Region 1*			*Region 2*		
	10 years ago	*Current*	*Change (%)*	*10 years ago*	*Current*	*Change (%)*
Wheat	17	8.15	-52.06	23	14.23	-38.13
Bajra	19.78	4.5	-77.25	20	9	-55
Jowar	7.86	2.8	-64.38	4	2	-50
Groundnut	13.3	3.65	-72.56	-	-	-
Cotton	21.55	8.00	-62.88	35	-	-100.0

Source: Field survey

The loss of agricultural productivity is severe in Region 1. The productivity of bajra and groundnut has decreased by more than 70 per cent and that of jowar and cotton has decreased by almost about 60 per cent. The productivity of wheat has almost become half. As reported, the farmers have stopped cultivating groundnut, mung, bajra and jowar. The impact also depends upon the wind that changes direction after every 6 months (as reported).

In Region 2, the farmers have reported for the increase in weeds and crop diseases. Due to industrial pollution (especially release of smoke), the farmers have stopped cultivating jowar, cotton and bajra. They are more interested in sowing short-term crops especially vegetables. According to them, banana and potato are not affected by pollution. Banana has hard flower and is not affected by smoke. In order to maintain the soil fertility, they sow banana and potato on alternate basis. The flowers of mango, drumstick and castor are highly affected by smoke.

7.4.2 *On Livestock*

The impact of pollution on livestock is reported at the time of survey. As shown in Fig. 7.3, more than 70 per cent of the households have responded for the impact of industrial pollution on livestock. The condition is severe in Region 1 as compared to Region 2. More than half of the respondents in Region 1 have reported for weakness, illness and decrease in quality as well as quantity of milk. In Region 1, more than 30 per cent have reported for unnatural deaths of their livestock. About 41 per cent in

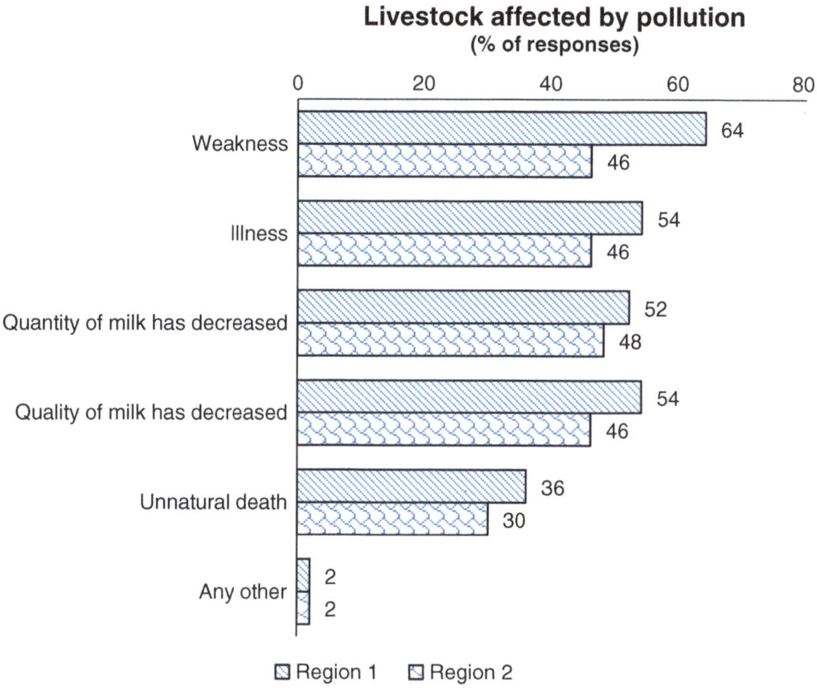

Fig. 7.3 Livestock affected by pollution (% of responses) *Source:* Based on field survey

Region 1 and 27 per cent in Region 1 have reported that the livestock productivity has decreased in the range of 50 to 100 per cent.

7.4.3 On Human Health

The industrial pollution is affecting the human health in one or the other way. The responses obtained from the field survey are presented in Fig. 7.4. The pollution-related diseases are found to be more in Region 1 as compared to Region 2. These responses are according to individual's perceptions which were cross-checked through doctor and sarpanch. About 52 per cent of the selected sample in Region 1 and 48 per cent in Region 2 have reported for per month health expenditure in the range of 10–20 per cent.

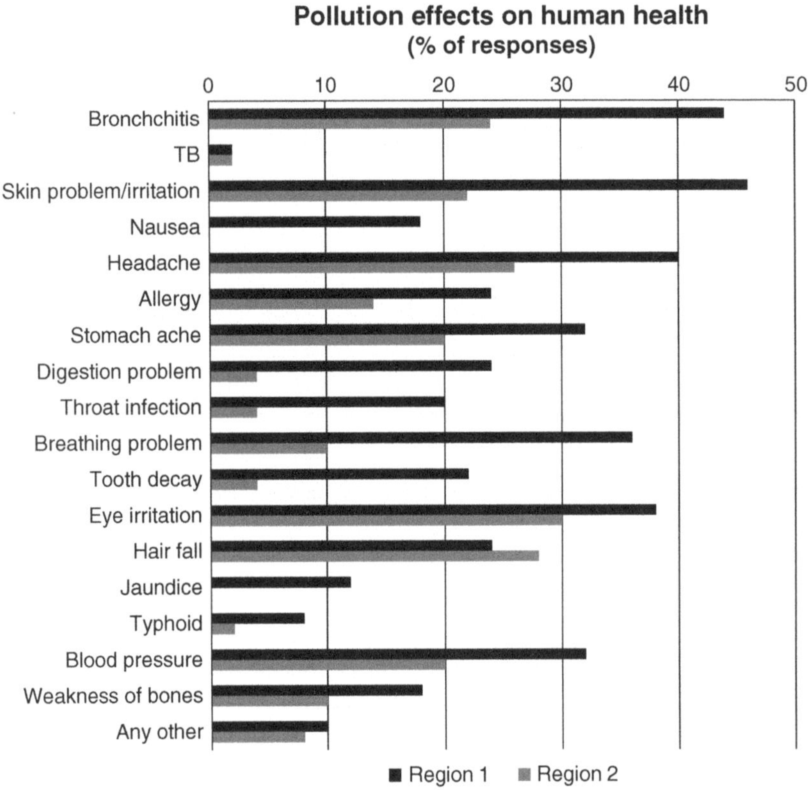

Fig. 7.4 Pollution effects on human health (% of responses) *Source*: Based on field survey

7.5 Estimated Results of Ordinary Logit Model

The results of the ordinal logit model are presented in Table 7.6 and the marginal effects of the change in probability of decrease in agricultural productivity due to one unit change in regressors are given in Table 7.7.

7.5.1 Demographic Characteristics

Belonging to a higher caste is not associated with decrease in agricultural productivity in Region 1 but some association is visible in Region 2. The

Table 7.6 Ordinal logit estimates

Variables		*Estimates*	
		Region 1	*Region 2*
Caste	=1	2.42	1.01
	=2	2.62	-3.30*
Age of the head farmer	=1	-5.02**	-3.33*
	=2	-6.96*	-2.22
Percentage of family members engaged in non-agriculture activity	=1	4.43	3.20
	=2	1.64	0.10
Percentage of female plus senior citizens engaged in agriculture	=1	8.03*	4.46*
	=2	7.26*	-1.79
Educational status	=1	9.84*	2.31**
	=2	3.80	1.03
Housing status	=1	5.22**	-6.53*
	=2	3.37**	-1.84
Awareness-generating assets owned by the household	=1	-6.95*	8.04*
	=2	-.47	2.65
Land size	=1	-2.78	3.25
	=2	0.37	2.12
Agricultural assets owned	=1	1.52	-0.95
	=2	5.90	-2.56
Source of irrigation	=1	3.64**	1.80
Industrial pollution	=1	15.92*	1.12**
	=2	4.48*	0.58**
Distance of village from the industry	=1	-5.81*	2.51
	=2	-8.31*	0.18
Threshold 1		6.80	1.50
Threshold 2		12.84	4.30
-2 log likelihood		42.89	62.01
Chi-square(df = 23)		51.45	41.89
McFadden R square		0.54	0.40
N		50	50

*Significance at 5 % level ($P \leq 0.05$) 95 %

**10 Significance at 10 % level ($P \leq 0.10$) 90 %.

Note: Threshold 1 and 2 are the intercepts for the second and third category, the intercept for the lowest category being normalized to zero

Source: Computed

marginal effects show that as one moves from a lower caste to a higher caste, the probability of decrease in agricultural productivity increases. This indicates that people belonging to higher caste are less concerned about the agriculture output as they have some other options. This shows

Table 7.7 Marginal effects of regressors on probability of decrease in agricultural productivity

Region	*Region 1*			*Region 2*		
	Low	*Moderate*	*High*	*Low*	*Moderate*	*High*
Constant	-0.146	-0.191	1.338*	-0.135	.988*	0.147
Caste	0.051	-0.068	0.017	-0.078*	-0.021	0.100*
Age of the head farmer	-0.045	0.01	0.035	-0.181*	-0.086*	0.267*
Percentage of family members engaged in non-agriculture activity	-0.058	0.243*	-0.185**	-0.060**	-0.026	0.086*
Percentage of female plus senior citizens engaged in agriculture	0.064	0.091	-0.156**	0.363*	0.108*	-0.471*
Educational status	0.14*	0.185*	-0.322*	0.015	0.009	-0.024
Housing status	0.091**	0.02	-0.112**	-0.104*	-0.062	0.166*
Awareness-generating assets owned by the household	-0.190*	-0.014	0.204**	0.176*	0.160*	-0.336*
Land size	-0.056	-0.094**	0.151*	-0.004	0.002	0.002
Agricultural assets owned	-0.084	0.105	-0.021	-0.025	-0.023	0.048
Source of irrigation	0.154	-0.047	-0.107	0.074	-0.031	-0.043
Industrial pollution	0.088*	0.148*	0.235*	0.11	-0.307***	0.197
Distance of village from the industry	-0.049	-0.163*	0.212*	0.095*	-0.04	-0.055

*Significance at 5 % level ($P \leq 0.05$) 95 %, **10 Significance at 10 % level ($P \leq 0.10$) 90 %.
Source: Computed

that agriculture is treated as the marginalized occupation. The age of the head farmer is likely to have a negative effect on decrease in agricultural productivity. This shows that the experience of the head farmer plays an important role in protecting the agricultural output from external risks.

The marginal effect has not shown a significant change in probability of decrease in agricultural productivity in Region 1 but it is found to be significant in Region 2. With the increase in age (i.e. the level of experience), the probability of decrease in agricultural productivity decreases.

7.5.2 Occupational Structure of the Household

The percentage of family members engaged in non-agricultural sector is not likely to have a significant impact on decrease in agricultural productivity in both the regions. However, the simultaneous effect in Table 7.7 show that with an increase in the engagement of family members in the non-agricultural sector, the probability of high decrease in agricultural productivity decreases in Region 1 by 19 per cent but increases in Region 2 by 9 per cent. Region 1 is highly backward with negligible opportunities in non-farm sector. With the increase in cost of agricultural production, more family members join the workforce. As a result, the probability of high decrease in agricultural productivity decreases. On the other hand, Region 2 is near the town. So adult males have lot of opportunities in the non-farm sector. This increases the probability of high decrease in agricultural productivity. The percentage of females plus senior citizens in agriculture increases the likelihood of decrease in agricultural productivity especially in Region 1. As the agricultural productivity decreases, instead of hiring labourers, females and senior citizens in the family join the workforce. The marginal effect of an increase in females and senior citizens in agriculture reduces the probability of decrease in agricultural productivity.

7.5.3 Status of the Household

A lower educational status of the household increases the likelihood of decrease in agricultural productivity. The marginal effects are significant in Region 1. For a low and moderate level, the probability of decrease in agricultural productivity is increasing, while for the high level, it is decreasing with increase in education. The population in the study villages is less educated with poor skill. When there is less decrease in agricultural productivity, they put more family labour to compensate for the cost of production. But when there is high decrease in agricultural productivity, even hard effort do not compensate losses. In Region 1, the decrease in agricultural productivity appears to increase with increase in housing status, while it is likely to decrease in Region 2. According to the marginal effects, in Region 1, with increase in housing status, the probability of decrease in agricultural productivity increases for the low category and decreases for the high category. In Region 2, the opposite is the case. Here the probability of decrease in agricultural productivity decreases for low category and increases for high category. In Region 1, with increase in housing status, the low decrease in agricultural productivity does not remain the major concern for the farmers. But a high decrease in agricultural productivity enforces the households to do more effort to check the rate of decrease in agricultural productivity. But in Region 2, a higher housing status releases the household members from agriculture to work in non-agricultural sector. Therefore, the rate of decrease in agricultural productivity increases. Awareness-generating assets owned by the households are likely to have negative effect on decrease in agricultural productivity in Region 1 and positive effect in Region 2. The marginal effect on probability of decrease in agricultural productivity decreases for the low category and increases for the high category in Region 1. Almost opposite is the case in Region 2. This is because of the difference in the availability of opportunities in both the regions. In Region 2, the farmers are able to explore more opportunities through awareness generating assets.

7.5.4 *Agricultural Status of the Household*

Land size and agricultural assets with the household do not appear to be related with decrease in agricultural productivity.

7.5.5 *Pollution-Related Variables*

Irrigation by well is likely to have a positive impact on decrease in agricultural productivity in Region 1. Industrial pollution increases the likelihood of decrease in agricultural productivity. The marginal effects show that with increase in industrial pollution, the probability of decrease in agricultural productivity increases.

Distance of village from the industry is likely to have a negative effect on the decrease in agricultural productivity especially in Region 1. As shown in Table 7.7, the probability of decrease in agricultural productivity decreases with distance for the moderate decrease and increases for the high decrease. The impact of water pollution occurs at shorter distance and that of air pollution occurs at longer distances. In Region 2, the distance of village from the industry is not found to have significant impact except for low category.

As a whole, the logit model shows that the increase in industrial pollution is likely to have an adverse effect on the agricultural productivity. The impact of industrial pollution is more in Region 1 as compared to Region 2. With the difference in the levels of development, proximity to town, levels of awareness and available opportunities, those variables that are effective in Region 1 becomes ineffective in Region 2 in subsidizing the decrease in agricultural productivity due to industrial emissions. Regarding the occupational structure of the study households, the percentage of family members engaged in non-agricultural activity and percentage of females plus senior citizens engaged in agriculture are able to reduce the probability of decrease in agriculture productivity in Region 1, but they increase the probability of decrease in agricultural productivity in Region 2. Similarly, in Region 1, education status and housing status of the household increase the likelihood of decrease in agricultural productivity, but the probability of high decrease in agricultural productivity decreases. In Region 2, these factors enable the person to find some better opportunity in the non-farm sector. An increase in housing status allows the cultivator to hire more labourers or giving the farm on contract. The decrease in the interest of the cultivator increases the probability of decrease in agricultural productivity. Among the pollution-related variables, irrigation by well has a greater likelihood of decreasing the agricultural productivity in Region 1. As reported, these industries, inject the untreated polluted water into the ground through percolation ponds. As a result, the underground water becomes toxic and unsuitable for irrigation. The results were found to be weak in Region 2 as effect varies according to the hydrological flows. Only the farmers of Ajod, Dashrath, Chhani and Omkarpura villages of Region 2 have reported for the contaminated underground water due to industrial pollution. The farmers of Bajwa village have left agriculture as the land became totally unproductive. The villagers of Kathi Devaliya and Kanalus in Region 1 have reported that they have lost their agriculture because of the polluted underground water. During the year 2012–13, their investment on agriculture was a complete failure as the seeds sown were burnt under the soil. The toxic slurry (containing gypsum and chalk) percolates through ponds and depletes the whole underground water. The underground water contains cadmium, cobalt, copper, zinc, lead and other heavy metals that destroys the agricultural productivity of land. The release of industrial smoke into the air (that contains oxides of sulphur) destroys the standing crops. Particularly, during the rainy season, the toxic contents in the smoke dissolve in the atmosphere and degrade the ambient air quality. Many of the mango trees do not bear fruits. If the flowering occurs, it does not stay for long. Due to the poor quality of grains, fruits and vegetables, the farmers do not get proper price in the market. The effect of pollution decreases if the distance of the village from the industry increases.

7.6 Conclusion

With the growth of industries, the agricultural productivity has declined in its surrounding villages. The impact of industrial emissions is more severe in the remote areas having population with less education and limited resources and negligible non-farm opportunities. With the decrease in agricultural productivity, these farmers, in order to reduce the cost of production, put more family labour in their farm. On the other hand, in the villages that are near to town, the households try to cover their agricultural losses by diversifying their economic activity. The decrease in agricultural productivity acts as a disincentive for farmers to invest in agriculture. As a result, the productivity further decreases. The industrial pollution has also affected the health of the livestock and decreased their productivity. The health of human being is also found to have come in the grip of industrial pollution.

The impact of industrial pollution in a region depends upon the type of pollutants released. But on comparing the two regions, it can be said that the depth of these effects are determined by other factors. Like for agricultural productivity, the number of years of experience of head farmer, education status of the household, housing status and awareness-generating assets are found to play an important role. The distance of the villages from the town is an indicator of accessibility to other options. The villages near the towns have higher proximity to basic services like education, health and communication, road as compared to the villages that are far off from the town. This is the reason why the depth of the impact of industrial pollution is less in Region 2 as compared to Region 1.

Therefore, in order to minimize the impact of pollution on social well-being, emphasis should be given to raise education level, generate awareness, media for sharing the experiences, development of basic services and employment opportunities.

Note

1. Bajwa village is very close to the selected industrial set-up of Region 2. However, it could not become the part of the study as there are no farmers currently. The land in this village has become totally unproductive, so the farmers had to leave agriculture.

References

Annual Survey of Industries, weblink: http://mospi.nic.in/
Census of India, Primary Census Abstract, 2001 and 2011.

CHAPTER 8

Summary, Conclusion and Policy Implications

Abstract This chapter concludes the study. The study considers that the inefficiencies in production processes generate negative environmental externalities. Maintenance of environmental standards is itself luxurious for India as it involves the cost of abatement technologies, monitoring equipment, etc. The factors like education, skill and infrastructural facilities improve with the process of development and contributes to increase in production efficiency and thus environmental externality. The study suggests some alternative measures that would increase the production efficiency on the one hand and would increase the social well-being on the other.

Keywords Summary · Conclusion · Policy implications

8.1 Summary

Trade liberalization has now achieved an important place in the growth policies of all the nations. Particularly, for the developing countries, the economic growth is more recognized in terms of its trade intensity and trade openness rather than its own inherent characteristics. It is now well accepted that the removal of trade barriers, on the one hand, increases the world output, enlarges consumption capacities and provides access to scarce resources and worldwide market for products which are essential for expanding the production activity for a nation. On the other hand, it

H. Jain, *Trade Liberalisation, Economic Growth and Environmental Externalities*, DOI 10.1007/978-981-10-2887-8_8

facilitates the sharing of knowledge, technical ideas and talents that supplement the growth process. On account of this, the country's mode of specialization, which was earlier used to depend upon its own resources and skill, is now determined by resources that it is able to access at competitive prices from the world. This increases the allocative efficiency as the increase in competition and economic integration shifts the resources from a less advantageous activity to a more advantageous one.

Due to improved access to intermediates, capital and FDI, not only the trade composition but also the structure of manufacturing industries of the developing countries has been altered. The developing countries, instead of exporting the primary goods, are now exporting the finished goods to developed countries. This implies that developing countries have now become the production base for finished goods. In order to compete in the world market, the developing countries aims at producing more export goods by substituting capital for labour.

The market is efficient when it is able to capture all types of associated costs and benefits. Taking into account the existence of environmental regulatory gaps between developed and developing countries, there is a high probability that on behalf of liberalization, the developed countries having stricter environmental norms might shift their pollution-intensive industries to developing countries having laxer environmental norms. Maintaining an environmental standard is luxurious for the developing countries as it involves abatement cost, monitoring costs as well as fines and penalties for crossing the permissible limits of emissions. Due to high competition in the world market, these countries generally focus on increasing their production by keeping their environmental standards low. Also there is high probability of FDI into polluting industries and the migration of pollution-intensive (or outdated) technologies to developing countries. The environmental pollution adversely affects the utility and well-being of the society. Since these costs are not captured by the market, they are referred to as externalities.

The study is focused on Indian economy that adopted trade liberalization policy in 1991. The liberal trade measures were implemented in a phased manner with a strong focus on manufacturing industries. It was held that manufacturing sector has strong inter-sectoral linkages. Its expansion would facilitate the growth of other sectors. More than two and half decades of experience show that after opening up the industries for trade and investment flows, Indian economy has achieved a remarkably high growth rate of 6 per cent per annum. It crossed the figure of 9 per cent per annum during 2003–04 to 2007–08. Manufacturing sector also crossed the 10 per cent mark during 2006–08. India's manufacturing sector currently contributes 17 per cent to GDP and nearly 80 per cent to merchandise exports. It shares about 79 per cent of total FDI in India.

India has comparative advantage in labour-intensive technologies, but the improved access to capital and FDI has made the Indian industries capital intensive. Capital-intensive techniques are generally pollution intensive. Thus increasing the scale of manufacturing output should mean higher pollution. On the contrary, an increase in income enables the country to adopt pollution control measures. Also the countries that are more open to trade can adopt clean technologies more quickly.
The study tries to answer the following questions:

1. Has India achieved its economic growth by specializing in pollution-intensive (low-technology) industries?
2. To what extent trade led high economic growth of India is able to shift the production activities to relatively clean technologies?
3. What type of effect these environmental externalities have on the well-being of the society?
4. Do the factors that improve with the process of growth have any role in normalizing the effect of environmental externality?

The study has the following objectives:

1. To study the growth and composition of Indian manufacturing industries after liberalization.
2. To examine the pollution effects of trade liberalization in terms of scale, composition and technique effects.
3. To determine the causes of growth of dirty industries in India.
4. To find the impact of environmental externalities on the human well-being.

Hypothesis

1. Trade liberalization has led to increase in production from pollution-intensive industries.
2. Trade liberalization has increased the exports from pollution-intensive industries.
3. Trade liberalization has increased the inflow of intermediates, capital and FDI into pollution-intensive industries.

4. Increase in domestic output shifts the production in favour of clean production process.
5. Environmental externalities affect the well-being of local people.

A large number of studies are available on income–environment relationship. The relationship of trade and environment has also been widely discussed. Since the nature of externalities and its impact on the society depends upon various socio-economic factors, considering those studies for the other economies will be illogical. Also India is a developing economy which predominantly has an agricultural base. Its own socio-economic structure, geographic characteristics, demographic structure and political conditions and the pace of improvement in the existing factors (education, skill, infrastructure, etc.) need special attention. Also the impact of environmental externality is higher at places where it is generated, and it decreases with distance. The investigation of these issues requires a micro level study.

In the present study, issues of trade liberalization, economic growth and environmental externalities with a focus on manufacturing industries are explored both at (a) macro level and (b) micro level. The macro level approach is based upon the secondary sources of data. The data for examining the post-liberalization trends of trade and investment flows and the resulting changes in growth and composition of manufacturing industries are collected from various official websites and reports like Annual Survey of Industries, WITS database, TPRI, Handbook of Statistics of Indian Economy (RBI), SIA Newsletter, DIPP, UNCTAD-TRAINS Database, Economic Surveys, DGCIS and Ministry of Commerce and Industry. The environmental externalities are determined in terms of pollution loads that are calculated on the basis of IPPS coefficients developed by the World Bank. Considering that pollution is a positive function of manufacturing output, the pollution loads are calculated with respect to output. All the monetary values were deflated for the year 2004–05. The industry-level data and pollution loads were obtained for 4 years – 1990–91, 1997–98, 2004–05 and 2009–10 – disaggregated at four-digit level as per NIC-2008. The data for different years were matched by concordance series. In order to know whether the highly producing industries are also the highly polluting industries, the industry-wise ranks of industrial output were compared with their pollution loads. The impact of trade induced manufacturing growth on environmental externalities is estimated in terms of scale effect, composition effect and technique effect. Scale effect is related to the increase in manufacturing output; composition effect reflects specialization achieved by the country and due to increased trade related activities; and the technique effect shows the impact of economic growth.

The micro level approach deals with investigating the impact of environmental externalities on the social well-being. Gujarat state has responded well to the trade liberalization policies and is known as the second highest industrialized state with higher FDI. On the basis of manufacturing output and pollution loads, two industries are selected for field survey: the petroleum refinery in Jamnagar, and fertilizer and chemical industry in Vadodara. The selected areas differ in terms of distance from the city, basic amenities and growth induced developmental factors. Since impact of environmental externalities decreased with increase in distance from industrial location, a survey was conducted in 10 villages surrounding each industry in a radius of 10 km. The selected sample consists of 50 households from each industrial location with the condition that they should have at least 20 years of experience of farming. Thus a purposive random sampling method was used. In order to capture the variations in social well-being, apart from pollution related variables, some other variables representing demographic characteristics, occupation structure and agricultural status were taken into account. This enabled us to capture the effect of other variables on social utility and well-being.

8.1.1 Findings

The study finds that under the various phases of trade liberalization measures in India, there has been significant decrease in tariff rates of almost all manufacturing products. Some of the products like minerals, machines and electricals, metals, chemicals and petroleum have experienced a sharp decline and are now facing the lowest amount of tariff (even less than 10 per cent). The tariff rates have significantly reduced for the semi-processed goods (from 12.2 per cent in 1990–91 to 9 per cent in 2010–11). The sharp decline in tariff rates for capital goods indicates improvements in access to capital from abroad. During the post-reforms, India has experienced a sharp increase in FDI (nearly 76 per cent in 2009–10) in gross investment; however, FDI inflows in manufacturing industries has shown a declining trend during the recent decade. The data show that most of the FDI is now moving into development of supporting sectors, particularly infrastructure and communication, as these sectors have a smoothening effect on trade flows of manufacturing industries. The industry-wise comparison of FDI supports this fact as the share of FDI has increased in electrical equipment (including S/W and Elec.), metallurgical industries and chemicals (other than fertilizers). Foreign technological collaboration is also high in these industries. It is to be noted here that the countries that are the major trading partners of India are showing the major amount of FDI. They are mainly the OECD nations. Owing to this, India's international trade (both exports and imports) have increased. More increase is observed in the imports of intermediates, capital goods and raw materials and exports of finished goods. Among the final goods, petroleum products have topped the export list followed by gems and jewellery, chemicals and related products. Among the import goods, petroleum, crude and products have topped the list, followed by gold and silver, mainly export related items and electronic goods. This is a clear indication that imports are meant mainly for boosting the production in those industries that have important place in exports. Among the top 10 trading partners, the scenario has now changed. During the 1990s, OECD nations were the major importing partners. Over the time, due to increase in demand for energy as well as rise in fuel prices, UAE has emerged as the second important import partner. The other OPEC nations have also now attained the top 10 positions in India's imports. The position of US, Germany, Japan and UK has gone down. Similar is the case with export partners. In 2012, UAE has emerged as the second most important export partner after US. The exports from OECD nations, viz., US, Japan, Germany, UK, Belgium and so on has decreased. China has now come in the top 10 ranking of India's trade partners. As a whole, India's growth experiences show that the trade related variables, viz., exports, imports, trade volume and FDI have contributed significantly after the reforms. But India's growth elasticity with respect to FDI is very high after a sufficient time lag, indicating its stronger effect in the long run.

Owing to trade liberalization measures in India, a significant change is observed in the structure of India's manufacturing industries. The capital–labour ratio has significantly increased over the period of two decades. The share of high technology and moderate technology industries in GVA has also increased. However, the value added per worker has not responded according to the increase in capital–labour ratio. This indicates an improper match between the imports of capital/technology and the skill of domestic labour. The industry-wise comparison of structural changes show that the growth rate of capital–labour ratio has increased particularly in low technology and moderate technology industries. FDI has increased in those industries that facilitate the production and transportation of finished goods. These are electrical equipment, computer, electronic and optical products, chemicals and chemical products and transportation. The relationship between trade liberalization, trade orientation and revealed comparative advantage show that tariff reduction is highly correlated with import penetration, RCA and GVA, indicating the export-oriented nature of trade measures. This has boosted the manufacturing output. The higher correlation between capital–labour ratio and export orientation show that production of manufacturing exports is based upon capital-intensive technology.

Further, in an attempt to determine the manufacturing growth and pollution concentration, it is observed that pollution load has significantly increased over the period of last two decades. From 2004/05 to 2009/10, the pollution load has increased at a rate of 24 per cent per annum, while during 1990/91 to 1997/98, it increased at a rate of 8 per cent per annum. Among the various pollutants, air pollution accounts for the major amount of industrial pollution in which SO_2 and NO_2 are the major pollutants. Surprisingly, the industry-wise distribution of pollution load shows that the number of polluting industries had decreased. The high value of standard deviation also clarifies that the pollution is distributed very unevenly among the manufacturing industries. According to the pollution loads of 2009–10, only around 12 industries are responsible for the highest amount of pollution. The rank correlation coefficient between the highly producing industries and the highly polluting industries has decreased over the period of time. This revealed that the increase in the scale of output is not a major contributor of pollution loads. This implies that some other factors are responsible for the increase in pollution loads. The study tries to capture those factors by taking a time dummy variable assuming that other factors like education, skill, infrastructure, communication and electricity supply improves with time. The regression results were obtained for both SO_2 and NO_2. Both linear and non-linear models were tried. It was observed that in the linear model scale effect is found to be stronger while the composition effect has a dampening effect. This implies that in the short run, an increase in scale of manufacturing increases the pollution load while the increase in capital–labour ratio has a diminishing effect. The non-linear model show that a further rise in scale of manufacturing activity has a negative and significant impact on pollution loads. The impact of income gains is found to be negative but insignificant. The combined effect of income gains and capital accumulation on pollution load is found to be positive and significant. This implies that the economic growth based on capital-intensive technologies is leading to environmental externalities. The time dummy is found to have a negative and insignificant effect. It is to be noted here that when the same variables were tried without the time dummy, the results were irrelevant and illogical. The inclusion of time dummy has increased the relevance of selected variables. The overall results of regression show that technique effect is weaker. Scale and composition effects are dominating the income effect. The inverted U-shape of the pollution loads with respect to manufacturing activity and continuous negative relationship of capital–labour ratio indicates inefficiency in the scale of production.

The impact of externalities on the well-being is investigated on the basis of field survey. The selected industries are highly growing industries and are well equipped with all the pollution control and monitoring equipment. It was found that these equipments are not operating on a regular basis. The farmers have reported that the emissions mainly take place through injecting untreated water into the ground, through percolation tanks digged in the periphery of the industry, releasing untreated water into the rivers/canals or by extending channels/pipelines/drainage lines that finally goes into the sea. Smoke is released especially when the weather is cloudy or at night. The responses obtained were cross-checked through schools, health centre and village officials.

Regarding the impact of pollution on agriculture, the villagers have reported for decline in quality of crop, burning of leaves and less flowering/falling of flowers as the common problem. The increase in cost of cultivation has made practicing agriculture less remunerative. The problem is found to be severe in Jamnagar than in Vadodara. The adverse impact on livestock and human health is also severe in Jamnagar as compared to Vadodara. It was reported that the health expenditure on account of industrial pollution has increased by around 10 per cent. The results of estimated model show that though industrial pollution is affecting the productivity, health and livestock in the villages surrounding the industrial location, but the severity of these impacts is associated with socio-economic factors. Similarly, for agricultural productivity, the number of years of experience of the head farmer, educational status of the family, housing status and awareness generating assets are found to play an important role. The distance of the village from the town indicates the accessibility to other options. The villages near the town have higher accessibility to basic services like education, health, communication, road, etc. as compared to villages that are far off from the town. This implies that with the development of socio-economic factors in the village near the industrial site, strength of the local population to mitigate risk of environmental externalities increases.

8.2 Conclusion

The trade liberalization process associated with industry-wise removal of trade barriers, inflows of FDI and change in composition and direction of trade reveals that the focus of reforms was biased towards those industries whose products have importance in exports for the developed countries. Improved access to capital- and skill-biased technologies has stimulated the growth of such industries. This has interacted with India's revealed comparative advantage and thus specialization in production activities. In this whole scenario, there was no concern about whether the local skill matches with the imported capital and technology. Also, adjustment of the foreign capital and technology with the local environment and their optimal use by the local manpower requires research and development. But India's expenditure on R&D is only 0.8 per cent of GDP, which is not sufficient for the foreign technologies to work in an efficient manner. Due to the inefficiencies in the production structure, the value added per worker is not responding according to the increase in capital and technology. The inefficiencies in production always results into inefficiencies in market, and when the cost of such inefficiency is not covered, they become externality which finally results into market failure. The study observed the environmental externalities due to increase in manufacturing activities in India. The pollution loads, particularly after 2004, increased at a high rate. However, the study rejects the significance of pollution havens hypothesis for India, which other studies have confirmed for the developing countries on account of differences in environmental standards between developed and developing countries. The decrease in correlation coefficient between manufacturing output and pollution load over the time indicates that the increase in pollution load is decreasing with increase in output. This itself indicates the impact of adjustment process between the worker and the technology. Thus the increase in industrial pollution loads is not due to inflow of capital-intensive technologies via trade liberalization, rather it is due to inefficiencies in production structure. Also the factors like education, skill and infrastructural facilities improve with the process of development and contribute to increase in production efficiency and thus decrease in environmental externality.

The existence of environmental externality adversely affects social well-being of population living in the vicinity of industrial sites by decreasing their agricultural productivity, livestock productivity, health, etc. The study finds that the risk due to environmental externality could be mitigated if the villages surrounding the industries are equipped with all the basic facilities and amenities. The increase in education, skill, awareness generating assets, employment opportunities, connectivity to town, etc. are some of the factors that empower the local population to overcome the risk of environmental externalities.

The study concludes that the maintenance of environmental standards is luxurious for India as it involves the cost of abatement technologies, monitoring equipment and so on. Also in competing at the global level, India has lost its focus on environmental quality. In this race of economic growth, there is a need to have some alternative path which would on the one hand, raise the industrial productivity and on the other hand would strengthen the population to maintain their social well-being by mitigating the risk.

8.3 Policy Implications

The study suggests the following measures:

(a) For industries

1. Increase in education and skill would enable the workers to understand the technologies quickly so as to make efficient use of them.
2. Before handling the technology, the workers should be trained about the ifs and buts of that technology.
3. Development of proper infrastructure is essential for raising production efficiency.
4. The producers as well as the workers should be made sensitive for environmental quality.

(b) For villages

1. Development of basic services, safe drinking water, sanitation and electricity is essential.

2. Improvement in basic amenities like school, health centres, road connectivity, communication facilities, awareness generating assets (e.g. television, mobiles), transportation facility and market plays an important role in generating awareness. This also empowers the local population to raise voices against pollution. If the local population is empowered, industrialists would themselves be careful.
3. The political lobbying between industrialists and villages should be controlled.
4. Influence of the industries in surrounding villages should be under the purview of their corporate social responsibility, not in terms of village administration or election of sarpanch.
5. It should be clear to villagers that the facility (if any) provided by the industries (e.g. schools, health centres, drinking water, community hall, roads, etc.) should not be at the cost of their environment.
6. Last but not the least, a proper harmony and transparency between villages and industrialists is essential to increase both private and social benefit.

ANNEXURES

A 3.1 QUESTIONNAIRE FOR FIELD SURVEY

1. Personal Information

1.1 Name: ______________________________ 1.2 Age: __________
1.3 Sex: Male/female 1.4 Caste: __________ 1.5 Phone no.______
1.6 Education level: Illiterate/primary/middle/secondary/higher secondary/graduate/postgraduate/professional degree or diploma
1.7 Village: ______________1.8 Taluka: ___________
1.9 District: ___________
1.10 Number of years of living in this village:
By birth/0–5 years/5–10 years/10–15 years/15–20 years/> 20 years

2. Family Information

Name of the family member	Age	Male/ female	Qualification	Relation with the respondent	Occupation	Annual income (Rs.)

Total family annual income (in Rs.): ____________________

H. Jain, *Trade Liberalisation, Economic Growth and Environmental Externalities*, DOI 10.1007/978-981-10-2887-8

3. Information about Ownership

3.1 Type of house: Own/rented

3.2 Nature of house: Kuchta/pucca/semi-pucca

3.3 Occupancy in house: One room/two room/three room/>three room/verandah/kitchen/outer space/bathroom/toilet/terrace/store room/washing space

3.4 Assets owned: Refrigerator/television/dish connection/cooler/AC/mobile/phone/gas connection/computer/internet/two wheeler/four wheeler/water purifier

4. Information about Agriculture Activities

4.1 How much agricultural land do you have?

(a) Up to 2.5 acre (marginal)

(b) 2.5 to 5 acre (small)

(c) >5 acre (large)

4.2 What type of crops do you cultivate?

a) Rabi: ________________________________

b) Kharif: ________________________________

c) Jayed: ________________________________

4.3 Kindly give detail about the crop and its productivity?

	Crop	Productivity
a)	____________	____________
b)	____________	____________
c)	____________	____________
d)	____________	____________
e)	____________	____________

4.4 How much is your annual agricultural income (in Rs.)?

a) Less than 20,000

b) 20,000–30,000

c) 30,000–40,000

d) 40,000–50,000

e) 50,000–60,000

f) More than 60,000

4.5 Indicate sources of irrigation.

a) Well/bore hole

b) Canal

c) River

d) Pond
e) Nala
f) Other (specify)

4.6 Agricultural assets owned:
a) Tractor
b) Pump sets (electric/diesel)
c) Plough
d) Land leveller
e) Pesticide pump
f) Thresher
g) Others____________________________

5. Information about Livestock

5.1 What type of livestock do you have? Specify their numbers.
(a) Cow ______
(b) Buffalo _______
(c) Goat ______
(d) Sheep_______
(e) Camel ___________
(f) Horse __________
(g) Ox_________
(h) Donkey________
(i) Any other___________

5.2 From where do you arrange the fodder for livestock?
(a) Self-arrangement from own field
(b) Purchase
(c) Take the animals for grazing
(d) Leave the animals for grazing
(e) Any other_____________________

6. Information about the Industrial Pollution

6.1 Do you have any information about the industry situated near by?
a) Yes
b) No

6.1.1 If yes, what is the name of the industry? ___________________

6.2 Do you have any information where industry disposes its waste?
a) Yes
b) No

6.2.1 If yes, please specify
- a) On the ground
- b) Water stream/river/pond
- c) By extending channel/drainage line to dispose off the waste at a distance
- d) Emission through chimney
- e) Any other__________________.

6.3 Do you know what types of pollutants are emitted by the industry?
- (a) Air: ____
- (b) Water: ____
- (c) Land: ____
- (d) Don't know

7. Regarding Impact of Industrial Emissions

7.1 On agriculture and livestock

7.1.1 Have you seen any major changes in agriculture production in past 10 years?

a) Yes b) No

7.1.2 If yes, of what type?

Type of changes in agricultural production	Yes	No
a) Production has decreased		
b) Quality of crops has declined		
c) Intensive cultivation (more use of fertilizer, insecticides and pesticides)		
d) Land productivity decreased		
e) More use of human power		
f) Fallow time period has decreased		
g) Fallow land has decreased		
h) Availability of fodder has decreased		
i) Any other		

7.1.3 How much decrease you have experienced in agricultural productivity?

Crop Productivity

	Current	5 years ago	10 years ago	15 years ago
a) ________	________	________	________	________
b) ________	________	________	________	________
c) ________	________	________	________	________
d) ________	________	________	________	________
e) ________	________	________	________	________

7.1.4 Have you seen any impact on the livestock health during past few years?
- a) Yes
- b) No

7.1.5 If yes, of what type?
- a) Weakness
- b) Illness
- c) Quantity of milk has decreased
- d) Quality of milk has decreased
- e) Unnatural death
- f) Any other

7.1.6 Kindly give detail about the decrease in livestock productivity.

	Current	5 years ago	10 years ago	15 years ago
a) Milk	________	________	________	________
b) Egg	________	________	________	________
c) Fish	________	________	________	________
d) Any other	________	________	________	________

7.1.7 Do you feel that industrial pollution is responsible for poor health of your livestock?
- a) Yes
- b) No
- c) Other (specify)

7.2 On health

7.2.1 Does any of your family member is suffering from any disease. If yes, of what type?

Name of the disease	Yes/No	Duration of disease	Number of visits to doctor
a) Bronchitis			
b) TB			
c) Skin problem/ irritation			
d) Nausea			
e) Headache			
f) Allergy			
g) Stomach ache			

(*continued*)

(continued)

h) Digestion problem
i) Throat infection
j) Breathing
k) Tooth decay
l) Eye irritation
m) Hair fall
n) Jaundice
o) Typhoid
p) Blood pressure
q) Weakness of bones
r) Any other________

7.2.2 What type of health problems the females are facing in the family?

____

____

____

7.2.3 How much amount of your family income do you spend on health?
a) 0–10%
b) 10–20%
c) 20–30%
d) 30–40%
e) 40–50%
f) >50%

8. Measures Taken Against Industrial Emissions

8.1 What necessary steps have you taken for prevention from pollution?
a) Medical care (doctor/vadiya/baba/self)
b) Started using filtered water/Bisleri/RO/RWHS
c) Use of face mask and gloves
d) Any other____________________

8.2 Have you done any complaint against the industrial pollution?
a) Yes
b) No

8.2.1 If yes, to whom?
a) The sarpanch/gram panchayat/government officer/media/etc.
b) Complain at the ministerial level
c) Agitation/lockouts/strike
d) Any other________________

8.3 How the action has been taken in this regard?
   a) The industry has ensured to use eco-friendly technology
   b) The industry has taken various environmental conservation steps under its CSR activities
   c) The industry has taken decision for regular maintenance and repairing of its plant and equipment
   d) The industry is providing medical facility to the local people
   e) Supply of safe drinking water
   f) The industry has planted various trees in its surrounding and also in the village to control the effect of pollution
   g) The government/gram panchayat has fixed strict environmental norms against the pollution (tax/fine/incentive/enforcement/ etc.)
   h) Any other_________________

8.4 What suggestions would you like to give to control the effect of pollution?
   a) Industry should be far off from the settlement
   b) Strict action should be taken against the industrial pollution
   c) The industrial activity should be stopped
   d) There should be timely maintenance and repairing of the plant equipment
   e) More plantations should be done
   f) Any other____________________

-X-

A 3.2 Distribution of Sample

District	Taluka	Villages	Sample size	Total
Jamnagar (Region 1)	Khambhaliya	Kathi Devaliya	5	50
		Vadinar	5	
	Jamnagar	Sapar	7	
		Gagva	2	
		Motikhavdi	5	
	Lalpur	Jakhar	9	
		Padana	4	
		Kanalus	7	
		Rangpar	6	
Vadodara (Region 2)	Vadodara	Dasharath	11	50
		Omkarpura	6	
		Chhani	7	
		Ajod	11	
		Ambika Nagar	6	
		Champapura	4	
		Dumad	5	

A 4.1 Average Tariffs and Peak Tariffs and Peak Tariffs for Industrial Products (1990–2012)

Tariff year	*Simple (in %)*	*Weighted (in %)*	*Peak tariffs (in %)*
1990	81.69	49.55	>200
1992	57.45	27.89	150
1997	30.08	19.92	85
1999	33	28.61	35
2001	31.06	24.76	30
2004	27.87	20.95	25
2005	15.38	11.97	15
2007	13.22	8.6	12.5
2008	9.1	5.91	10
2009	9.43	7.21	8.6 (2009–10)[a]
2011	13.7	7.7	2.2
2012	13.7	6.75	1

[a]WTO Secretariat Calculation.

Source: World Integrated Solutions and various economic surveys.

A 4.2 Trends in Composition of Merchandise Exports (Post-Reform)

Year/commodity	*1990–91*	*1997–98*	*2004–05*	*2011–12*
I Primary products	23.83	21.96	16.22	14.97
IA Agriculture and allied products	18.49	18.93	10.14	12.29
IB Ores and minerals	5.34	3.03	6.08	2.68
II Manufactured goods	71.62	75.83	72.70	61.34
IIA Leather and manufactures	7.99	4.73	2.90	1.57
IIB Chemicals and related products	9.52	12.56	14.90	12.21
1. Basic chemicals, pharmaceuticals and cosmetics	6.81	8.06	8.55	8.03
2. Plastic and linoleum products	0.61	1.47	3.63	2.09
3. Rubber, glass, paints, enamels and products	1.71	2.03	2.11	1.57
4. Residual chemicals and allied products	0.39	0.99	0.61	0.53
IIC Engineering goods	12.40	15.24	20.77	22.03
1. Iron and steel	0.89	2.50	4.69	2.12
2. Manufacture of metals	2.51	2.92	4.07	3.16
3. Machinery and instruments	3.84	3.42	4.45	4.72
4. Transport equipment	2.21	2.65	3.39	6.87
5. Electronic goods	1.28	2.17	2.19	2.92
6. Other engineering goods	1.67	1.58	1.97	2.25
IID Textile and textile products	23.93	25.85	16.23	9.19
1. Cotton yarn, fabrics, made-ups, etc.	6.45	9.32	4.13	2.23
2. Natural silk yarn, fabrics, made-ups, etc., including silk waste	0.72	0.50	0.48	0.07
3. Manmade yarn, fabrics, made-ups, etc.	1.25	2.30	2.35	1.66
4. Manmade staple fibre	0.00	0.05	0.11	0.19
5. Woollen yarn, fabrics, made-ups, etc.	0.07	0.31	0.08	0.05
6. Readymade garments	12.32	11.07	7.85	4.50
7. Jute and jute manufactures	0.92	0.53	0.33	0.15
8. Coir and coir manufactures	0.15	0.20	0.13	0.07
9. Carpets	2.06	1.56	0.76	0.28
IIE Gems and jewellery	16.11	15.27	16.47	15.40
IIF Handicrafts (excluding handmade carpets)	1.23	1.50	0.45	0.08
IIG Other manufactured goods	0.43	0.67	0.98	0.85
III Petroleum products	2.88	1.01	8.37	18.22
IV Others (all commodities)	1.67	1.20	2.71	5.48

Source: Computed from DGCIS

A 4.3 Trends in Composition of Merchandise Imports (Post-Reform)

Year/commodity	*1990–91*	*1997–98*	*2004–05*	*2011–12*
I Bulk imports	25.70	35.65	38.02	43.89
IA Petroleum, crude and products	14.28	19.68	26.76	31.66
IB Bulk consumption goods (cereals and cereal preparations, edible oils, pulses, sugar)	1.32	3.58	2.78	2.37
IC Other bulk items	10.10	12.40	8.48	9.85
1. Fertilisers	2.33	2.69	1.23	2.35
2. Non-ferrous metals	1.45	2.22	1.17	1.00
3. Paper, paper boards, manufactures including news prints	0.60	1.21	0.65	0.53
4. Crude rubber, including synthetic and reclaimed	0.30	0.39	0.37	0.51
5. Pulp and waste paper	0.60	0.68	0.44	0.28
6. Metalliferous ores, metal scrap, etc.	2.02	1.78	2.21	2.73
7. Iron and steel	2.79	3.43	2.39	2.45
II Non-bulk imports	31.32	64.35	61.98	56.11
IIA Capital goods	13.82	23.61	22.54	20.30
1. Manufactures of metals	0.40	0.78	0.82	0.88
2. Machine tools	0.62	1.02	0.56	0.61
3. Machinery except electrical and electronics	4.97	8.73	6.11	6.18
4. Electrical machinery except electronics	2.25	0.91	1.07	0.98
5. Electronic goods	0.00	5.03	8.96	6.66
6. Computer goods	0.00	0.41	0.60	0.33
7. Transport equipment	2.20	2.53	3.88	2.87
8. Project goods	3.37	4.19	0.53	1.79
IIB Mainly export-related items	8.72	16.66	15.33	11.13
1. Pearls, precious and semi-precious stones	4.93	8.06	8.45	6.23
2. Organic and inorganic chemicals	3.02	7.13	5.11	3.87
3. Textile yarn, fabrics, made-ups, etc.	0.58	0.99	1.41	0.79
4. Cashew nuts	0.18	0.50	0.36	0.23
IIC Others	8.79	24.07	24.11	24.69
1. Gold and silver	0.00	7.64	10.00	12.53
2. Artificial resins and plastic materials, etc.	1.45	1.67	1.31	1.54
3. Professional, scientific controlling instruments, photographic optical goods	1.40	1.80	1.37	1.08
4. Coal, coke and briquettes, etc.	1.04	2.87	2.87	3.56
5. Medicinal and pharmaceutical products	0.62	0.94	0.63	0.61
6. Chemical materials and products	0.38	0.72	0.73	0.71
7. Non-metallic mineral manufactures	0.27	0.33	0.42	0.42
8. Others	3.64	8.10	6.77	4.24

Source: Computed from DGCIS

A 4.4 Direction of India's Trade

Year	*1990–91*			*1997–98*			*2004–05*			*2009–10*		
Country/region	*Export*	*Import*	*Trade*	*Export*	*Import*	*Trade*	*Export*	*Import*	*Trade*	*Export*	*Import*	*Trade*
OECD countries	56.5	57.2	56.9	55.7	51.4	53.4	43.7	35.9	39.2	36.0	32.8	34.0
All EU countries	27.5	29.4	28.6	26.1	25.7	25.9	21.0	16.8	18.6	20.2	13.3	15.9
Belgium	3.9	6.3	5.3	3.5	6.4	5.1	3.0	4.1	3.6	2.1	2.1	2.1
France	2.4	3.0	2.7	2.2	1.9	2.0	2.0	1.7	1.8	2.1	1.5	1.7
Germany	7.8	8.0	7.9	5.5	6.1	5.8	3.4	3.6	3.5	3.0	3.6	3.4
Italy	3.1	2.5	2.8	3.2	2.2	2.7	2.7	1.2	1.9	1.9	1.3	1.6
Netherlands	2.0	1.8	1.9	2.3	1.1	1.6	1.9	0.7	1.2	3.6	0.7	1.8
UK	6.5	6.7	6.6	6.1	5.9	6.0	4.4	3.2	3.7	3.5	1.5	2.3
North America	15.6	13.4	14.4	20.7	10.0	14.9	17.5	7.0	11.5	11.6	6.6	8.5
Canada	0.9	1.3	1.1	1.2	1.0	1.1	1.0	0.7	0.8	0.6	0.7	0.7
US	14.7	12.1	13.3	19.4	9.0	13.8	16.5	6.3	10.6	10.9	5.9	7.8
Asia and Oceania	10.4	11.2	10.9	6.9	9.0	8.0	3.5	6.4	5.2	2.9	6.8	5.3
Australia	1.0	3.4	2.4	1.3	3.6	2.5	0.9	3.4	2.3	0.8	4.3	3.0
Japan	9.3	7.5	8.3	5.4	5.2	5.3	2.5	2.9	2.7	2.0	2.3	2.2
Other OECD countries	3.0	3.2	3.1	2.0	6.8	4.6	1.7	5.7	3.9	1.3	6.0	4.2
Switzerland	1.2	1.1	1.2	1.0	6.4	3.9	0.6	5.3	3.3	0.3	5.1	3.3
OPEC	5.6	16.3	11.7	10.1	22.7	16.9	15.8	9.0	11.9	21.1	32.1	27.9
Indonesia	0.6	0.3	0.5	1.2	1.8	1.5	1.6	2.3	2.0	1.7	3.0	2.5
Iran	0.4	2.4	1.5	0.5	1.5	1.1	1.5	0.4	0.8	1.0	4.0	2.9
Iraq	0.1	1.1	0.7	0.0	0.4	0.3	0.2	0.0	0.1	0.3	2.4	1.6
Kuwait	0.2	0.8	0.6	0.5	5.5	3.2	0.5	0.3	0.4	0.4	2.9	1.9

(*continued*)

(continued)

Year	*1990–91*			*1997–98*			*2004–05*			*2009–10*		
Country/region	*Export*	*Import*	*Trade*	*Export*	*Import*	*Trade*	*Export*	*Import*	*Trade*	*Export*	*Import*	*Trade*
Saudi Arabia	1.3	6.7	4.4	2.0	6.0	4.2	1.7	1.2	1.4	2.2	5.9	4.5
UAE	2.4	4.4	3.5	4.8	4.3	4.5	8.8	4.2	6.1	13.4	6.7	9.3
Eastern Europe	17.9	7.8	12.1	3.7	2.7	3.1	2.1	2.3	2.2	1.0	2.1	1.7
Romania	0.3	0.1	0.2	0.0	0.1	0.1	0.1	0.2	0.1	0.0	0.0	0.0
Russia	16.1	5.9	10.3	2.7	1.6	2.1	0.8	1.2	1.0	0.5	1.2	1.0
Developing countries	17.1	18.7	18.0	29.5	23.2	26.1	37.8	25.7	30.9	39.3	32.6	35.2
Asian Countries	14.4	14.0	14.2	22.8	17.5	19.9	29.9	20.2	24.4	29.9	25.7	27.3
SAARC	2.9	0.5	1.6	4.6	0.6	2.4	5.3	0.9	2.8	4.7	0.6	2.1
Afghanistan	0.0	0.0	0.0	0.0	0.0	0.0	0.0	0.0	0.0	0.3	0.0	0.1
Bangladesh	1.7	0.1	0.8	2.2	0.1	1.1	2.0	0.1	0.9	1.4	0.1	0.6
Bhutan	0.0	0.0	0.0	0.0	0.0	0.0	0.1	0.1	0.1	0.1	0.1	0.1
Maldives	0.0	0.0	0.0	0.0	0.0	0.0	0.1	0.0	0.0	0.0	0.0	0.0
Nepal	0.3	0.2	0.2	0.5	0.2	0.3	0.9	0.3	0.6	0.9	0.2	0.4
Pakistan	0.2	0.2	0.2	0.4	0.1	0.2	0.6	0.1	0.3	0.9	0.1	0.4
Sri Lanka	0.7	0.1	0.4	1.4	0.1	0.7	1.7	0.3	0.9	1.2	0.1	0.5
Other Asian developing countries	11.4	13.5	12.6	18.2	16.9	17.5	24.6	19.4	21.6	25.2	25.1	25.2
China	0.1	0.1	0.1	2.1	2.7	2.4	6.7	6.4	6.5	6.5	10.7	9.1
Hong Kong	3.3	0.7	1.8	5.5	0.8	2.9	4.4	1.6	2.8	4.4	1.6	2.7
South Korea	1.0	1.5	1.3	1.3	2.4	1.9	1.2	3.1	2.3	1.9	3.0	2.6

Malaysia	0.8	2.3	1.7	1.4	2.8	2.2	1.3	2.1	1.7	1.6	1.8	1.7
Singapore	2.1	3.3	2.8	2.2	2.9	2.6	4.8	2.4	3.4	4.3	2.2	3.0
Thailand	1.4	0.3	0.7	1.0	0.6	0.8	1.1	0.8	0.9	1.0	1.0	1.0
African Countries	2.2	2.4	2.3	4.7	4.3	4.5	5.4	3.5	4.3	5.8	4.3	4.9
Benin	0.1	0.0	0.0	0.1	0.0	0.0	0.1	0.1	0.1	0.1	0.0	0.1
Egypt	0.5	0.2	0.3	0.7	0.5	0.6	0.5	0.1	0.3	0.8	0.6	0.7
Kenya	0.2	0.1	0.1	0.4	0.1	0.2	0.5	0.0	0.2	0.8	0.0	0.3
South Africa	0.0	0.0	0.0	0.0	0.0	0.0	1.2	2.0	1.6	1.2	2.0	1.7
Sudan	0.1	0.0	0.1	0.1	0.0	0.1	0.4	0.0	0.2	0.3	0.2	0.2
Tanzania	0.2	0.1	0.2	0.2	0.2	0.2	0.2	0.1	0.2	0.5	0.1	0.2
Zambia	0.1	0.4	0.3	0.1	0.2	0.2	0.1	0.0	0.0	0.0	0.0	0.0
Latin American countries	0.5	2.3	1.5	2.0	1.4	1.7	2.6	1.9	2.2	3.6	2.6	3.0
Others/unspecified	2.9	0.0	1.3	1.1	0.0	0.5	0.5	27.2	15.8	2.5	0.4	1.2
Total	100.0	100.0	100.0	100.0	100.0	100.0	100.0	100.0	100.0	100.0	100.0	100.0

Source: *Handbook of Statistics on Indian Economy*, RBI.

Classification of Manufacturing Industries by Technology Group

High-technology manufacturing

- Division 21 Pharmaceuticals
- Division 26 Computers, electronic and optical products
- Group 30.3 Air spacecraft

Medium high-technology manufacturing

- Division 20 Chemicals
- Group 25.4 Weapons and ammunition
- Division 27 Electrical equipment
- Division 28 Machinery
- Division 29 Motor vehicles
- Division 30 X 30.1 30.3 Transport equipment excluding ships, boats, excluding air and spacecraft
- Group 32.5 Medical & dental instruments

Medium low-technology manufacturing

- Group 18.2 Reproduction recorded media
- Division 19 Coke and petroleum products
- Division 22 Rubber and plastic products
- Division 23 Other non-metallic mineral products
- Division 24 Basic metals
- Division 25 X 25.4 Fabricated metal products excluding machinery
- Group 30.1 Ships and boats
- Division 33 Repair and installation machinery

Low-technology manufacturing

- Division 10 Food
- Division 11 Beverages
- Division 12 Tobacco
- Division 13 Textiles
- Division 14 Clothing
- Division 15 Leather products
- Division 16 Wood products
- Division 17 Paper products

- Division 18.1 Printing
- Division 31 Furniture
- Division 32 X 32.5 Other manufacturing excluding medical and dental instruments

Source: UNIDO's elaboration based on UNIDO (2012)

Index

H. Jain, *Trade Liberalisation, Economic Growth and Environmental Externalities*, DOI 10.1007/978-981-10-2887-8

Q

R

The manufacturer's authorised representative in the EU is Springer Nature Customer Service Centre GmbH, Europaplatz 3, 69115 Heidelberg, Germany. If you have any concerns regarding our products, please contact ProductSafety@springernature.com

Printed and bound by CPI Group (UK) Ltd, Croydon, CR0 4YY
30/09/2026
02225443-0001